FUNDAMENTALS
of
GENEALOGICAL
RESEARCH

FUNDAMENTALS
of
GENEALOGICAL
RESEARCH

by

Laureen Richardson Jaussi

Gloria Duncan Chaston

Special Contributors

Cynthia Mallory Trunnell

Beryl Putnam Duffin

PUBLISHED BY

DESERET BOOK COMPANY

SALT LAKE CITY, UTAH

1966

Library of Congress No. 66-26091

Copyright 1966

DESERET BOOK COMPANY

Lithographed by

DESERET-news PRESS

in the United States of America

To Our Husbands

August W. Jaussi

and

A. Norton Chaston

Who have encouraged us in this writing and who were
our first genealogical instructors.

PREFACE

This book is written for the many individuals who are willing and want to complete their own genealogical research and as an introduction to a systematic approach to genealogical research. It can be used as a textbook and as a reference volume. If an individual will select one genealogical problem and search each record source in the order suggested, he will build a foundation for orderly research procedures on any problem; he will also learn when to eliminate or to alter certain procedures. It is expected that the individual will use this book as a reference, and thus eliminate the need to memorize many technicalities, allowing him more time for analysis. The technicalities may then be learned gradually as he gains experience in the record sources.

It is intended that this book will encourage those with L.D.S. ancestry to search the records of the L.D.S. Church jurisdiction. The L.D.S. Church pioneers did not conduct extensive genealogical research and did not preserve genealogical data in the present family group record form; as a result family records in the possession of the present generation are frequently inaccurate and incomplete.

Much of the information in this book on L.D.S. Church records has not previously been published; however, it is realized that this information is only a beginning and that further research and writings in L.D.S. Church records is desirable.

Those who cannot use the facilities of the library of The Genealogical Society, or one of its branches, should study Chapter 20 prior to reading Chapter 12.

The authors wish to express their appreciation to those under whom they have studied genealogical research: David E. Gardner, David H. Pratt, J. Grant Stevenson, Norman E. Wright, and the late Archibald F. Bennett.

Laureen Richardson Jaussi
Gloria Duncan Chaston

TABLE OF CONTENTS

SECTION I
THE GENEALOGICAL RESEARCH METHOD

Chapter   Page

SECTION II
GENEALOGICAL RESEARCH TOOLS

Chapter   Page

SECTION IV

LIST OF FIGURES AND CHARTS

Page

CHARTS

SECTION I

THE GENEALOGICAL RESEARCH METHOD

Chapter One

INTRODUCTION

It is often stated that the only way to learn genealogical research is to do it. This belief could be more truthfully stated, "The only way to learn genealogical research is to do it *correctly*." To do it correctly one needs a detailed knowledge of the genealogical research method, and he needs to apply this knowledge by searching the records. To learn the theory and memorize the details does not make one a genealogical research specialist. Both theory and practice are involved in genealogical research; readings, lectures, and study complement the practical application.

By definition, genealogy is the study of individual or family descent with particular emphasis on names, places, dates, and relationships. Genealogical research is the method used to identify individuals by searching records and evaluating evidence. As a guide in genealogical research, a scientific or systematic method is employed. Thus, *scientific genealogical research* is systematic investigation into original records and primary sources to determine correct names, places, dates, and relationships pertaining to each individual ancestor and all members of his family.

The genealogical research method helps the individual control his research rather than the research control the individual by introducing systematic steps and procedures to be used as guides in the solution of genealogical problems.

The genealogical research method includes three basic steps: (1) selecting an objective, (2) searching the records, and (3) evaluating the evidence. These steps are followed in all research problems whether they deal with the individual or the family. Each time evidence is evaluated, a new objective is selected, additional records are searched, and another evaluation is made.

The genealogical research method involves searching sources pertinent to the research objective, not necessarily all known sources, but those which have been determined to be the best and the most reliable sources for the time period and locality in question.

The genealogical research method requires a detailed knowledge of the elements of identity: names, places, dates, and relationships. In genealogical research one searches a particular record, for a particular name, in a particular locality, for a particular period of time, and establishes relationships of one individual to another.

The genealogical research method employs certain tools. These research tools should not be confused with the research method and are used as aids to the method. The genealogical researcher finds The Family Record Book is an aid in organizing and preserving pedigree charts and family group records; notekeeping is an aid in recalling what records have been searched and what information was or was not found; libraries are an aid in storing genealogical source material; and family organizations are an aid in combining research time and money.

The genealogical research method requires that one work from the known to the unknown as in other scientific research. Since the researcher is best acquainted with himself, the first step is to place his own name on a pedigree chart and record identifying data. The pedigree chart published by The Genealogical Society of The Church of Jesus Christ of Latter-day Saints, Inc. (Genealogical Society) is recommended for this beginning step.

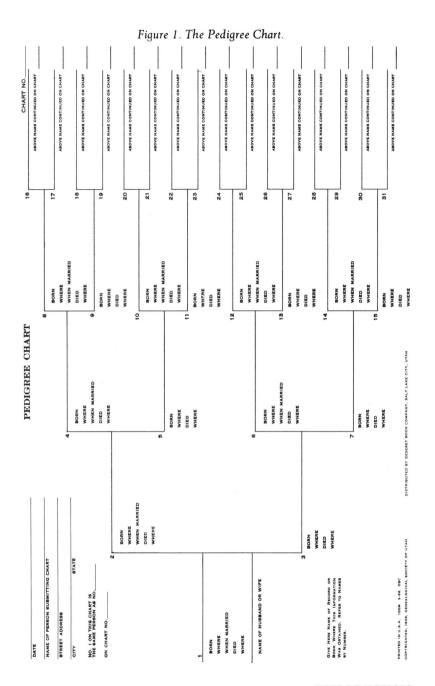

Figure 1. The Pedigree Chart.

Figure 2. The Family Group Record.

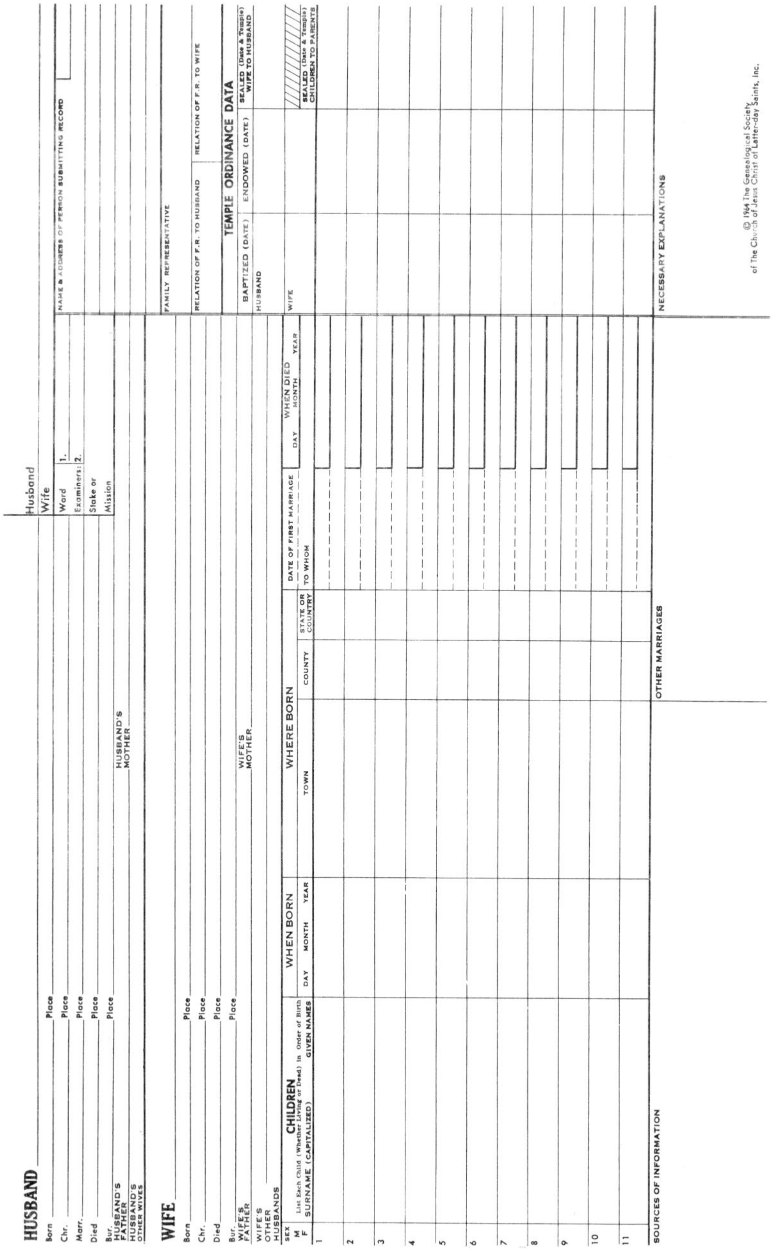

HUSBAND

Born — Place

Chr. — Place

Marr. — Place

Died — Place

Bur. — Place

HUSBAND'S FATHER — HUSBAND'S MOTHER

HUSBAND'S OTHER WIVES

WIFE

Born — Place

Chr. — Place

Died — Place

Bur. — Place

WIFE'S FATHER — WIFE'S MOTHER

WIFE'S OTHER HUSBANDS

Husband

Wife

Ward 1.

Examiners: 2.

Stake or Mission

NAME & ADDRESS OF PERSON SUBMITTING RECORD

FAMILY REPRESENTATIVE

RELATION OF F.R. TO HUSBAND — RELATION OF F.R. TO WIFE

TEMPLE ORDINANCE DATA

	BAPTIZED (DATE)	ENDOWED (DATE)	SEALED (Date & Temple) WIFE TO HUSBAND
HUSBAND			
WIFE			

SEX M F	CHILDREN List Each Child (Whether Living or Dead) in Order of Birth SURNAME (CAPITALIZED) GIVEN NAMES	WHEN BORN DAY	MONTH	YEAR	WHERE BORN TOWN	COUNTY	STATE OR COUNTRY	DATE OF FIRST MARRIAGE TO WHOM	WHEN DIED DAY	MONTH	YEAR	SEALED (Date & Temple) CHILDREN TO PARENTS
1												
2												
3												
4												
5												
6												
7												
8												
9												
10												
11												

SOURCES OF INFORMATION

OTHER MARRIAGES

NECESSARY EXPLANATIONS

© 1964 The Genealogical Society of The Church of Jesus Christ of Latter-day Saints, Inc.

The second step is to record one's name on the family group record for his immediate family. The family group record published by The Genealogical Society is recommended.

After the first family group record has been completed and verified, one should proceed to the next generation, completing and verifying family group records for each ancestral couple.

The genealogical research method is most successful when a uniform system is used for recording information on family group records and pedigree charts. For members of The Church of Jesus Christ of Latter-day Saints (L.D.S. Church) certain standards of uniformity have been outlined in the *Genealogical Instruction Manual*.[1] There is one section devoted to each element of identity (names, places, dates, and relationships) and several sections on miscellaneous items necessary for submitting family group records to The Genealogical Society. The *Genealogical Instruction Manual* contains information that is not repeated in this textbook, and should, therefore, be used as a companion reference.

The genealogical research method emphasizes quality rather than quantity. One judges the quality of research by the sources listed on the family group record and the pedigree chart. Care is taken to document in detail the sources from which the information was compiled.

The genealogical research method involves two phases of activity: (1) the survey phase and (2) the research phase. The same basic steps are included in the survey phase of each pedigree and family group problem and the steps include searching the home jurisdiction, printed secondary records, and the L.D.S. Church jurisdiction; organizing and evaluating the results of these searches; and choosing a new objective preparatory to the research phase. The survey phase is explained and outlined in detail in this textbook.

The research phase involves a detailed understanding of the records, procedures, and techniques peculiar to each geographic area of the world and can be learned by studying a more detailed textbook on research of the specific locality.

---

[1]The Genealogical Society of The Church of Jesus Christ of Latter-day Saints, Inc., *Genealogical Instruction Manual* (Salt Lake City: 1965).

PROJECT ASSIGNMENTS

1. Obtain a copy of the *Genealogical Instruction Manual.*

2. Begin the pedigree chart. Record your name on line 1.

3. Begin family group records for the first four generations shown on your pedigree chart. Record only information found in your own home.

Chapter Two

ELEMENTS OF IDENTITY

■ Names, places, dates, and relationships are elements of genealogical identity. One element, e.g., names, cannot stand alone in a record as a sole means of identification as frequently different individuals have the same names. Two persons in the same community may have the same name and may have been born about the same time, in which case relationships are necessary to identify one individual from the other. Thus, all four elements of identity are required for the proper identification of an individual.

NAMES

Origin: Prior to 1265, English and European pedigrees show names of individuals by only one given name, and not until the latter part of the thirteenth century and into the fourteenth century are persons identified by two names, a given name and a family or surname.

When studying the origin of surnames, it becomes apparent that because of the nature of their acquisition, persons bearing identical surnames are not necessarily blood relatives. And, conversely, members of the same family may have different surnames.

Early surnames were acquired or inherited from (1) places, (2) occupations, (3) ancestry, and (4) personal characteristics.

1. Place surnames often originated from a man's place of residence or geographic location such as a hill, brook, forest, woods, lake, or town. A man could have been called "John of the Hill," "John by the Water," John of Middleton," or "John of Cheshire." Later the name may have been shortened or changed to John Hill, John Bywater, John Middleton, or John Cheshire.

At the time surnames originated, most persons could not read or write, and residences, inns, and shops displayed signs denoting the name of the establishment; usually the signs showed an object (bell), animal (fox), or bird (swan). Individuals who lived or worked at these places often acquired their names from them: John of the Bell, Henry at the Fox, and William Swan.

2. Occupational surnames were acquired as a result of an individual's vocation or occupation. In English they include Baker, Carpenter (German, Zimmerman; Swedish, Snedker), Taylor, Cook, Smith (German, Schmidt; French LeFevre or LeFeure), and Clark (from the English pronunciation of clerk).

3. Ancestral or patronymic surnames originated from the name of an ancestor, generally from the father's given name, e.g., John, whose father was William, may have been known as John, son of William. Later the name may have been shortened to John Williams, or John Williamson, the "s" or "son" being substituted for "son of." Other names with a prefix or suffix indicating "son" or "son of" are the Irish, O' (O'Neil); German, sohn or son (Mende'ssohn); Russian, ov, ovich, or ovitch (Ivanov, Ivanovich); Scandinavian, sen or son (Jensen or Johansson); Norman, Fitz (Fitzgerald); Gaelic, Mac (Mac Donald); Hebrew, ben (Solomon ben David); Saxon, ing (Harding); and Welsh, ap (ap Rice or Price). The anglo-saxon "son" was added to abbreviations of names as well as full names. For example, son of David could be Dawson, Davison, or Davidson. When the Welsh "ap" was used before a name beginning with a vowel, often the "a" was dropped and the

"p" was added to the beginning of the name, i.e., ap Richard became Pritchard or ap Howell became Powell.

Many families adopted these ancestral surnames as the family or clan name, and used them as established surnames in the following generations. Others, including Scandinavians, Welshmen, and some Dutchmen practiced patronymics (giving a child a given name plus a surname—the surname being the given name of the father or sometimes the grandfather) and consequently the surname changed every generation. For example, Johannes Arvidsson was the son of Arvid Nilsson, and Arvid Nilsson was the son of Nils Jonsson.

4. Personal characteristic surnames were acquired as a result of the individual's physical appearance or personal title and include such names as Little, Tall, Black (German, Schwartz), Armstrong, King, Knight, and Noble.

Customs and Traditions: People in many countries write their names with given name first, then middle name, and surname last; others take exception to this rule. The Chinese write their family name (or surname) first, then a generation name taken from a poem, and the given name, last. People from Spanish speaking countries often have compound surnames—the child having been given a surname taken from the surname of both of his parents, grandparents or relatives. If the name is from both parents, the given name is recorded first, the father's surname next, and the mother's surname last.

Traditions or customs of certain families or nations in naming of children often are clues in establishing relationships and extending pedigrees. In some countries, families name the first boy after the paternal grandfather, the first girl after the maternal grandmother, the second boy after the maternal grandfather, the second girl after the paternal grandmother, the third boy after his father, and the third girl after her mother. Other children born in the family are often named after aunts, uncles, or other relatives.

Many parents have given their children one name and then proceeded to call them by another name, e.g., William, Bill; Richard,

Ricky, or Dick; Robert, Bob; Thomas, Tom; Edward, Ed, or Eddy; Kathryn, Kate, or Kay; Elizabeth, Liz, Betty, or Betsy; Mary, Mally, Molly, or Polly; Margaret, Peggy; Rebecca, Becky to mention a few. This practice is hundreds of years old, and being aware of it helps a researcher to reconcile discrepancies in names.

There are some names which are not necessarily nicknames, but synonymous names: John-Ian; Donald-Daniel; Jean-Jane-Janet-Jessie; Bessy-Betsy-Betty-Elizabeth; Isabel-Isabella-Elizabeth; Alexander-Alisdair; McKinnon-Love; McDonald-Donaldson; Robertson-MacRoberts or Roberts-Robb-Robertson-Robinson; and Steven-Stevenson-Stein-Steinson are just a few.

Changes in Names: There are various reasons why people change their names, and these changes are confusing to a genealogical researcher. When moving from one country or colony to another, some individuals change their names to conform to the new language, e.g., Stina Maja to Christina Maria; Schmidt to Smith; or Rosenberger to Rose. Many persons anglicize their names after immigrating to the United States. Other changes are a result of dialect and phonetic spellings, e.g., Becker to Baker. Slaves and domestic help adopt names from their masters and landowners; thus a noble name does not necessarily mean ancestry from a noble family. The nationality of the surname does not necessarily indicate the nationality of the individual, e.g., a German family surnamed Zweig (meaning Branch) moved to a French colony in Louisiana and changed their name to the French "LeBranche."

There are persons who have aliases and persons who have legally changed their names through adoptions or for other personal reasons. There are instances when a person's name is not always recorded the same way, e.g., Mary Ann Long may be written Mary Long, Ann Long, M. A. Long, Mary A. Long, or M. Ann Long.

Spelling variations: There is no particular standard for spelling names, and the same name may be found spelled more than one way in a single document. A person who cannot read or write cannot give the correct spelling of his name nor check to see if his name is being written accurately by another person. A recorder does not always know if he is spelling a name correctly, and even the informant who can read and write is not always aware of how his name is being recorded.

Spelling variations are problems to the genealogical researcher when searching indexes or alphabetized lists of names. A name with several spellings may be easily overlooked unless the researcher uses his imagination and searches for every possible spelling of each name. One should be aware that different vowels have similar sounds and are often interchanged in the spelling of names. Consonants may be either single or double and sound the same. Note the following spelling variations for the same surnames:

Trippess	Tripos
Trippes	Treppass
Tripess	Trepass
Trippus	Tripas
Trippuss	Trepas
Trippos	Trappes
Dixon	Dixsone
Dixone	Dickson
Dixson	Dikeson
Smith	Psmythe
Smithe	Psmithe
Smythe	Psmyth
Smyth	Schmidt
Psmith	
White	Wight
Whit	Whight
Whyte	Wyte
Wite	Wighte

Dialect, which is more of a problem in some geographic areas than others, may alter the sound of a name, e.g., the "h" sound may be silent or an "r" sound may be added in the pronunciation. The name of Allibone has been spelled in the following ways:

Allibone	Halebone
Alibone	Hallebone
Allebone	Ellerbone
Alebone	

PLACES

The place of residence or the place where an event occurred is an important element of identity as the genealogical research method involves searching for names in specific places. The same types of problems are encountered when trying to identify or establish places as when trying to identify or establish names. Maps, atlases, gazetteers, directories, and dictionaries are aids in solving place name problems and are particularly useful for establishing the correct town, county, and state as detailed on the family group record.

Spelling Variations: Phonetics can be a problem in identifying place names even though there are standard ways of spelling places. Some recorders had never heard of some of the names of places pronounced to them by the informant, or they did not know the correct spelling and were left to their own discretion to spell the names of places as best they could: Cogenhoe as Cocknoe; Bubbenhall, Bubnell; Warwickshire, Warricksher; Worcestershire, Woostasher or Woostersher; Edinburgh, Edinburro; Tooele, Toowilla; Sacandaga, Sakundawga; and Lockhurst Lane, Lockers Lane.

Errors in Names of Places: Problems arise in names of places as a result of (1) names given erroneously for places that never existed, (2) names given of actual places, but the ancestor never resided there, (3) interpretation of handwriting or copy errors, and (4) boundary and/or name changes. The first situation could be a result of phonetics, misinformation (unintentional or deliberate), or lack of geographic knowledge, i.e., correct town, but incorrect county; or correct state, but incorrect county. There are several reasons for naming an incorrect extant place: the name of a nearby larger city may be mentioned rather than the name of the smaller, less known town; the event may have occurred in a locality other than the usual residence; or a port of embarkation may have been mentioned as a place of residence. Copy errors often occur, e.g., Darley Dale as Darby Dale. Frequently locality boundaries have changed, names of places have changed, jurisdictions have changed, and record repositories have changed.

DATES

To solve genealogical problems the researcher searches for a particular name in a particular place at a particular period of time. The particular period of time to search can be indicated in a number of ways: a given date, a year calculated from an age at a dated event, or a period of time approximated or estimated from other clues. When searching for information where an actual date is given, the usual time period allowed for possible error is five years prior to, and five years after the assumed date, making a total of eleven years to search. Searches for dates in some situations often cover a much longer period of time.

Months Indicated by Numerals: There is no worldwide or nationwide standard as to the method of recording dates when numerals are used to indicate months. Frequently the day is recorded first; at other times the numeral indicating the month is recorded first. A date written 6-7-1850 could be interpreted as June 7, 1850 or 6 July 1850. A date recorded as 28-7-1850 is correctly interpreted as 28 July 1850 since there are no months numbered above 12. When searching a list of dates, the day column can easily be determined if there are numbers higher than 12.

Hints for Recording Dates: When interpreting and recording dates, a good habit to form is that of writing the day first, then the month by name, followed by the year, i.e., 7 October 1929. By following this procedure, the month separates the day and the year, and there is less chance of misinterpretation than when the month is recorded first, then the day, and the year. Likewise, by writing the month out rather than using a number, there is no question as to which month is being referred to. Another precautionary measure is to write legibly and clearly. January, when abbreviated to Jan. can easily be mistaken for June, as could June for Jan. and May for Mar. or vice versa. Some numbers that are easily mistaken for one another are 7 and 2, 7 and 9, 4 and 7, 1 and 7, 6 and 4, 5 and 8, 5 and 3, and 3 and 8. Each country and nationality has its own writing idioms which may require some study, e.g., the Norwegian 7 is written with a line through it. A Scottish or English 7 often looks like a 4 and is frequently interpreted as such.

RELATIONSHIPS

Relationships must be combined with names, places, and dates in order to establish the correct identity of an individual. When more than one person with the same name is residing in the same community at the same period of time, lives to maturity, and has offspring, the only way to properly identify each individual is to establish correct relationships. Other problems in establishing correct relationships are often a result of misinterpretation and miscalculation, incorrect use of terminology, assuming non-existent relationships, belief in traditions that cannot be proven, and desire to be related to famous persons.

Lines of Responsibility: The responsibility for each individual member of The Church of Jesus Christ of Latter-day Saints is to have his own pedigree as complete and as far back as possible with a corresponding ancestral family group record for every marriage union on the pedigree. When one thinks of the requirement of a family group record for each ancestral couple, the task of genealogical research is not so overwhelming as when gathering information about collateral relatives or people who happen to have the same surnames as one's direct ancestors.

Each line of ancestry is of equal importance, i.e., it is just as necessary to complete research for a maternal great grandmother as it is for a paternal great grandfather. A person may by choice prefer to do research on one particular line, but this does not change the responsibility of completing a family group record for each marriage union on the pedigree. *The responsibility begins with oneself by completing and verifying all information about one's own family, then proceeding to the previous generation and concentrating on finishing one family group record at a time and extending the pedigree a generation at a time.*

To compile a correct pedigree, one traces his blood ancestry; however, because of the possibility of adoptions, illegitimate births, infidelity, or promiscuity on the part of an ancestor, one can never know if his pedigree is accurate. When some children are adopted, their birth certificates are completed or changed to conform with the adoption, and the adopted parents are listed as father and mother on the birth certificate. There is no indication that the parents are not the natural, or blood, parents, and the certificate is considered valid by law. In L.D.S. families a sealing line may be different from a blood line, in which case the *Genealogical Instruction Manual* should be consulted.

Calculation of Relationships: To identify each individual in his proper place on family group records and pedigree charts, correct relationships must be established. There are lineal, brother-sister, and collateral relationships. A lineal relationship is a relationship between individuals in a direct line of descent from a common ancestor, e.g., father to son. A brother-sister relationship is a relationship between individuals descended from the same parents. A collateral relationship is a relationship between two individuals having a common ancestor, but the lineal descent from that common ancestor is different, e.g., cousins, aunts, and uncles.

The following methods of calculating and interpreting relationships are those recommended by The Genealogical Society of The Church of Jesus Christ of Latter-day Saints, Inc.

Lineal relationships are those lines of ancestry shown on a standard pedigree chart. The following pedigree illustrates the relationship of one's ancestors to oneself.

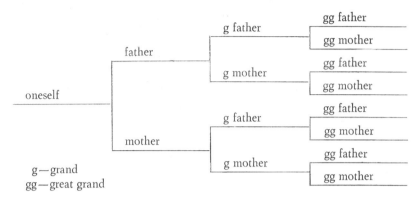

Figure 3. Lineal Relationships.

In the following pedigree, the relationship of oneself to his ancestors is illustrated. The terminology is reversed, i.e., oneself is a son to his father, grandson to his grandfather, etc. The Family Representative in the L.D.S. Church usually calculates the relationship from himself to the ancestor.

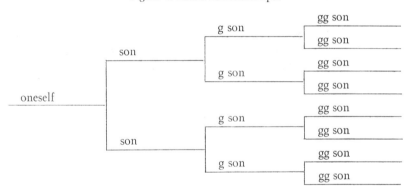

Figure 4. Lineal Relationships.

To calculate collateral relationships between individuals, one first determines the correct lineal relationship from each individual to the common ancestor. The children of a husband and wife are brothers and sisters. The children of brothers and sisters are first cousins. The children of first cousins are second cousins.

Figure 5. Collateral Relationships.

George Green — Isabell James

William Green	— brothers —	Jonathan Green
David Green	— 1st cousins —	Thomas Green
Israel Green	— 2nd cousins —	Peter Green
Thomas Green	— 3rd cousins —	Archibald Green

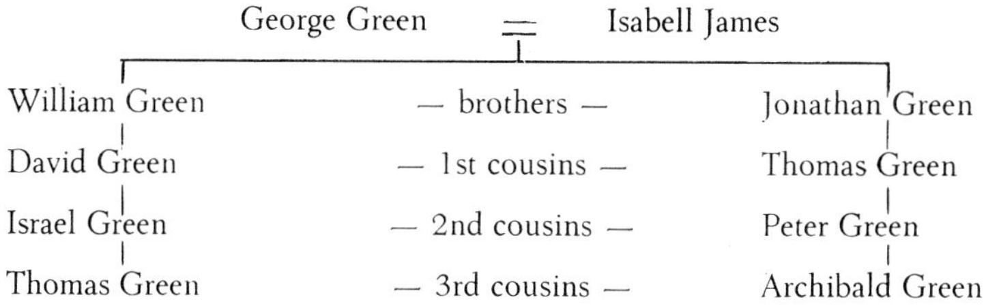

Full cousins are those that are descended in equal numbers of generations from the common ancestor. When generations are not equidistant from the common ancestor, the number of unequal generations is referred to as "removed."

Figure 6. Collateral Relationships.

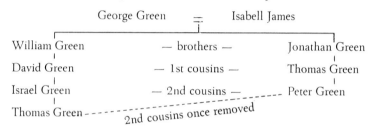

George Green — Isabell James

William Green — brothers — Jonathan Green
David Green — 1st cousins — Thomas Green
Israel Green — 2nd cousins — Peter Green
Thomas Green — 2nd cousins once removed

The brothers and sisters of an individual's parents are aunts and uncles to that individual. The children of one's brothers and sisters are nieces and nephews.

Figure 7. Collateral Relationships.

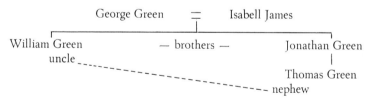

George Green — Isabell James

William Green — brothers — Jonathan Green
uncle

Thomas Green
nephew

The brothers and sisters of an individual's grandparents are grandaunts and granduncles to the individual. The grandchildren of one's brothers and sisters are grandnieces and grandnephews.

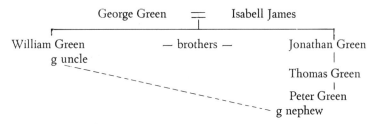

Figure 8. Collateral Relationships.

The brothers and sisters of an individual's great grandparents are great grandaunts and great granduncles to the individual. The great grandchildren of one's brothers and sisters are great grandnieces and great grandnephews.

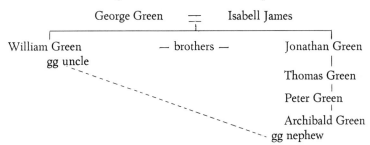

Figure 9. Collateral Relationships.

There are several types of charts available to help one calculate collateral relationships. (See *Genealogical Instruction Manual.*) However, one must know the lineal descent of the individuals from the common ancestor before these charts can be used. These charts generally depict the closer, most often calculated relationships, and are limited in the number of relationships they show.

PROJECT ASSIGNMENTS

1. Make a list of possible spelling variations for surnames on your pedigree.

2. Record names, places, dates, and relationships on the pedigree chart and family group records selected in Chapter 1 as detailed in the *Genealogical Instruction Manual.* Use maps, atlases, gazetteers, and/or directories to establish the correct place names.

Chapter Three

THE ORIGIN AND CLASSIFICATION
OF RECORDS

■ After the genealogical researcher has selected a research objective, he searches specific records which he feels may accomplish the objective. There are specific records to be searched in the survey phase of genealogical research and specific records to be searched in the research phase. All records originate in four jurisdictions and are classified in twelve record categories. Certain jurisdictions initiate records in several categories, and conversely, a record category could contain records from several jurisdictions. Figure 10 illustrates the relationship of record categories to jurisdictions.

JURISDICTIONS

The authority or governing body which initiates the keeping of certain records is referred to as a "jurisdiction." For convenience in conducting genealogical research these authorities or jurisdictions are as follows: (1) home jurisdiction, which includes any record that originates in the home; (2) ecclesiastical (church) jurisdiction, which includes records kept by any and all religious denominations; (3) civil (government) jurisdiction, which includes records originating as a result of government authority; and (4) social and commercial jurisdiction, which includes all records except those originating in the home, ecclesiastical, or civil jurisdictions.

Figure 10. Relationship of Record Categories to Jurisdictions.

Record Categories	Home Juris-diction	Ecclesi-astical (church) Juris-diction	Civil (gov't) Juris-diction	Social & Com-mercial Juris-diction
Home Records	X			
Printed Secondary Records	X	X	X	X
Ecclesiastical (church) Records		X		
Vital (civil) Records			X	
Cemetery Records	X	X	X	X
Census Records			X	
Land Records			X	
Probate Records		X	X	
Court Records		X	X	
Military Records			X	
Emigration-Immigration Records			X	X
Social & Commercial Records				X

RECORD CATEGORIES

Similar or like records are grouped in categories for convenience in studying and searching the records.

Home Records

Record Categories	Home Juris-diction	Ecclesi-astical (church) Juris-diction	Civil (gov't) Juris-diction	Social & Com-mercial Juris-diction
Home Records	X			

The home, as a record category, contains information from the home jurisdiction, e.g., family Bible records, diaries and journals, photographs, letters, and scrapbooks.

Printed Secondary Records

Record Categories	Home Jurisdiction	Ecclesiastical (church) Jurisdiction	Civil (gov't) Jurisdiction	Social & Commercial Jurisdiction
Printed Secondary Records	X	X	X	X

This record category refers to compilations made from other records, hence, the term "secondary" records. They are in printed form and originate in each of the four jurisdictions. The home often initiates printed family histories and genealogies; churches often publish a record of memberships or meetings; and civil authorities issue reference material in the form of maps, printed surveys, directories, etc. The majority of printed secondary records of value to the genealogical researcher are from the social and commercial jurisdiction, e.g., publications of patriotic societies; histories and periodicals published by historical societies; gazetteers, atlases, and directories published by commercial firms; and textbooks and manuals published by genealogical firms.

Ecclesiastical (Church) Records

Record Categories	Home Jurisdiction	Ecclesiastical (church) Jurisdiction	Civil (gov't) Jurisdiction	Social & Commercial Jurisdiction
Ecclesiastical (church) Records		X		

By definition this record category contains only records initiated by the ecclesiastical jurisdiction, i.e., records initiated by any and all religious denominations. The types of records originating in the different churches vary with each religious group and might include records of meetings, records of membership, records of ordinances, financial records, etc. Most often one thinks of the church initiated parish registers of baptisms (christenings), marriages, and burials, as the minister or clerk usually records the christening or baptism date rather than the birth date since he is present for the former rather than the latter. Likewise, the burial date rather than the death date is usually recorded in church records as a church official officiates the day of the funeral but is not likely to be present at the death.

Vital (Civil) Records

Record Categories	Home Juris- diction	Ecclesi- astical (church) Juris- diction	Civil (gov't) Juris- diction	Social & Com- mercial Juris- diction
Vital (civil) Records			X	

This record category is reserved for the records of birth, marriage, death, and divorce kept by authorities in the civil jurisdiction, or government, and does not include information from the ecclesiastical jurisdiction.

Cemetery Records

Record Categories	Home Juris- diction	Ecclesi- astical (church) Juris- diction	Civil (gov't) Juris- diction	Social & Com- mercial Juris- diction
Cemetery Records	X	X	X	X

Cemetery records orginate in all four jurisdictions. There are family burial plots, church cemeteries, government cemeteries and cemeteries owned by social and commercial organizations. This record category includes mausoleum and sexton's records, burials, epitaphs, tombstone inscriptions, etc.

Census Records

Record Categories	Home Juris- diction	Ecclesi- astical (church) Juris- diction	Civil (gov't) Juris- diction	Social & Com- mercial Juris- diction
Census Records			X	

This record category includes census records initiated in the civil jurisdiction.

Land Records

Record Categories	Home Juris-diction	Ecclesi-astical (church) Juris-diction	Civil (gov't) Juris-diction	Social & Com-mercial Juris-diction
Land Records			X	

Records concerning land transactions most often originate in the civil jurisdiction and include abstracts of title, contracts, deeds, leases, plat books, tax records, surveys, transfers, etc.

Probate Records

Record Categories	Home Juris-diction	Ecclesi-astical (church) Juris-diction	Civil (gov't) Juris-diction	Social & Com-mercial Juris-diction
Probate Records		X	X	

Probate records originate in either the civil or ecclesiastical jurisdictions depending upon the locality and period of time. Wills, letters of administration, accounts and settlements, testaments, etc., are included in this record category.

Court Records

Record Categories	Home Juris-diction	Ecclesi-astical (church) Juris-diction	Civil (gov't) Juris-diction	Social & Com-mercial Juris-diction
Court Records		X	X	

Civil and ecclesiastical jurisdictions initiate records in this category, e.g., affidavits, calendars, case files, journals, summonses, writs, citizenship, etc.

THE ORIGIN AND CLASSIFICATION OF RECORDS

Military Records

Record Categories	Home Jurisdiction	Ecclesiastical (church) Jurisdiction	Civil (gov't) Jurisdiction	Social & Commercial Jurisdiction
Military Records			X	

Records concerning military service, e.g., service, pension, and veteran files, and selective service records are included in this category and are usually initiated by the civil jurisdiction.

Emigration-Immigration Records

Record Categories	Home Jurisdiction	Ecclesiastical (church) Jurisdiction	Civil (gov't) Jurisdiction	Social & Commercial Jurisdiction
Emigration-Immigration Records			X	X

The civil jurisdiction and the social and commercial jurisdiction initiate emigration-immigration records which include shipping, passenger, debarkation, and embarkation lists; maps; passports; etc.

Social and Commercial Records

Record Categories	Home Jurisdiction	Ecclesiastical (church) Jurisdiction	Civil (gov't) Jurisdiction	Social & Commercial Jurisdiction
Social & Commercial Records				X

The social and commercial record category includes only records from the social and commercial jurisdiction, e.g., records of private schools, social and professional organizations, insurance companies, hobby groups, and patriotic societies.

The foregoing explanation of jurisdictions and record categories is not limited to one geographic location, but is representative of jurisdictions and record categories used in genealogical research in all geographic areas. It is also representative of both the survey phase and research phase. The survey phase of genealogical research as discussed in this textbook is limited to the home jurisdiction, printed secondary records (all jurisdictions), and the L.D.S. Church jurisdiction.

Figure 11. Record Categories and Jurisdictions in The Survey Phase

Record Categories	Home Jurisdiction	Ecclesiastical (church) Jurisdiction	Civil (gov't) Jurisdiction	Social & Commercial Jurisdiction
Home Records	X			
Printed Secondary Records	X	X	X	**X**
Ecclesiastical (church) Records		L.D.S.		
Vital (civil) Records				
Cemetery Records				
Census Records				
Land Records				
Probate Records				
Court Records				
Military Records				
Emigration-Immigration Records				
Social & Commercial Records				

Chapter Four

THE ORIGIN AND EVALUATION
OF EVIDENCE

■ In the previous chapter, jurisdictions are explained as the authority that initiates records. Genealogical information contained in these records is known as genealogical evidence. As genealogical evidence accumulates, its effect upon the genealogical problem is known as proof. In this chapter, genealogical evidence is explained in relation to the type of testimony, type of written record, and source of testimony.

In a court of law the most desirable evidence is the testimony of a living personal witness. The genealogical researcher cannot produce a living, personal witness to verify every genealogical item on the pedigree chart and family group record. Evidence given by other than a living personal witness, and this includes written records where the informant was a personal witness, but not present to give oral testimony, is classified by the court as hearsay evidence. The court will accept genealogical facts based upon the most reliable hearsay evidence, but genealogical fact cannot be proven to absolute certainty. The genealogical researcher must be satisfied with proof by a "preponderance of evidence," which is simply proving a case by presenting enough evidence to convince the court or jury. The civil courts will accept a "preponderance of evidence," because it is impossible to reconstruct any genealogical event and prove the facts "beyond a shadow of a doubt."

The genealogical researcher should consider himself judge and jury as he weighs each genealogical fact. Is the evidence admissable? Is it reliable? Who was the informant? Is the source primary or secondary? Has all the available evidence been presented? The answers to these questions require training and logical thinking.

For the purpose of evaluation, the genealogical researcher finds it convenient to classify evidence as either direct or circumstantial. In order to do this the research problem must be carefully defined, as all evidence has a direct bearing on some problem somewhere. The evidence must be weighed in the light of one genealogical fact at a time.

Direct evidence is information which answers a problem directly or which aids in a conclusion concerning a disputed issue.

Circumstantial evidence is information which does not give a direct answer to a problem, but, with some inferences and calculations, implies a certain answer or gives clues which might lead to more direct evidence.

ORAL TESTIMONY

All evidence of value to the genealogical researcher has its origin in personal witness and memory. When an event occurs the persons participating in the event are personal witnesses to its occurrence. The retelling of the details by word of mouth results in oral testimony. For example, in a marriage ceremony the bride, groom, and minister are considered participants in the event; the guests are considered personal witnesses. When information concerning the ceremony is repeated orally by these participants or witnesses from their memory, it becomes oral testimony.

DOCUMENTARY TESTIMONY

When oral testimony is written or recorded, it becomes documentary testimony. In the previous example concerning a marriage ceremony, the minister, bride, and groom are most likely to participate in a written record of the event. However, it is possible that guests also might make a written record of the event in letters, journals, or newspaper items.

When dealing with documentary testimony one must consider the possibility of an error or an omission by the recorder which may not be intentional, but may be due in part to mispronunciations or misunderstandings.

Documentary testimony, or written records, are classified by type:

Original Records: An original record contains the first recording of an event in a particular record according to law or custom. Details of an event can be recorded in more than one original record. The death of an individual could be recorded in the family Bible, on a death certificate, in the minister's burial book, in the cemetery records, and in the records of the funeral director. These are all original records because each is the first recording of the event in a particular type of record.

A photocopy of an original record is considered the same as the original because the possibility of a copying error has been eliminated.

Copied Records: In genealogical research it is not always possible to obtain the original record, and photocopies are expensive. For this reason the majority of written records used by the genealogical researcher are copied from the original records by the custodian of the records, the researcher, or an agent.

There are varying degrees of copied records. If a copy is made of a copied record, the result is another copied record. The first copy will have gone through the copying stage only once, while the second will have gone through the copying stage twice, and the possibility of error or omission increases with each copy.

SOURCE OF TESTIMONY

In genealogical research many records are searched, each of which may make a valuable contribution to completing a family group record or extending a pedigree. However, as information is obtained from the records, it will be noted that discrepancies (conflicting information) occur. It is, therefore, necessary to analyze each item of information as to witness and time element, and to classify the source of testimony as primary or secondary.

The source of testimony is judged by (1) whether the informant was a participant or an eye-witness to the event, and (2) whether the information was given at or near the time of the event.

Primary Source: A primary source is testimony of an event by a participant or an eye-witness of the event given at or near the time of the event.

Secondary Source: A secondary source is testimony of an event by someone other than a participant or an eye-witness, or is testimony given by a participant or an eye-witness at some time after the event when the fallibility of memory could be a factor.

A secondary source is not necessarily inferior to a primary source, but to classify the source of testimony as secondary should increase the genealogical researcher's awareness of the possibility of error.

Each item of genealogical information must be considered separately. It is not always correct to say, "This record is a primary source," or "This record is a secondary source," but rather, "All the information recorded in this record is *from* a primary source; all of the information is *from* a secondary source; or some of the information is *from* a primary source and some is *from* a secondary source."

In summary, there are two types of testimony, oral and documentary. Documentary testimony can be further classified as (1) original records and (2) copied records. Whether the testimony is oral or documentary and the record is original or copied, the source of *each item* of genealogical data must be analyzed to determine whether it is from a primary or secondary source. To be considered a primary source the informant must have been closely associated with the event and must have given the information shortly after the event occurred, otherwise it is secondary. It is not always possible to determine the identity of the informant or the date the information was given; but, as the genealogical researcher becomes familiar with record sources and their history in various geographic areas, he will learn to analyze specific records when the informant or time element is uncertain.

1. Oral testimony
   a. Primary source
   b. Secondary source

2. Documentary testimony
   a. Original records
      (1) Primary source
      (2) Secondary source
   b. Copied records
      (1) Primary source
      (2) Secondary source

EVIDENCE
(Direct)
(Circumstantial)

SOLVING DISCREPANCIES

As the genealogical researcher searches record sources and evaluates the resultant evidence, he often finds that information in one source does not agree with that in another concerning the same event or individual. One person is not always responsible for providing the information in every record source. Not only do the informants vary, but the circumstances of recording vary, resulting in discrepancies. Obviously, before there can be a discrepancy, evidence must be obtained from at least two different sources.

When discrepancies occur, the genealogical researcher must determine which record to accept as the most reliable. There is no quick and sure answer. However, if the researcher considers the following items, he will have a basis upon which to begin to solve discrepancies:

1. Search the records. Have all record sources been searched which are likely to contain the most pertinent information for the

present pedigree problem? In the survey phase this includes the home jurisdiction, certain printed secondary records, and all L.D.S. Church records which could possibly contain information on the problem.

2. Determine the type of record. Is it the original record, or could it contain copying errors and omissions?

3. Evaluate the source of the testimony. Is it possible to identify the informant? Was the informant closely associated with the event? Was the information given at or near the time of the event?

4. Analyze each item of evidence. Does the evidence have a direct bearing on the problem or does it imply or suggest certain answers?

5. Prove or disprove the clues and suggestions obtained through circumstantial evidence by searching records containing direct evidence.

6. Compare and evaluate all present evidence.

7. Accept the results of evaluation.

In addition to the items mentioned in this chapter, the genealogical researcher should learn the circumstances and customs surrounding the making of each record, which will not be apparent until the researcher studies the history and content of the records in each particular locality of research.

PROJECT ASSIGNMENT

1. Classify as to source of testimony (primary or secondary) the evidence used in compiling the family group records for the first four generations of ancestry.

SECTION II

GENEALOGICAL RESEARCH TOOLS

Chapter Five

THE FAMILY RECORD BOOK

■ The Family Record Book, sometimes referred to as the Book of Remembrance, is a genealogical research tool used to organize and preserve both unfinished and finished pedigree charts and family group records and could contain any number of items such as photographs, newspaper clippings, biographies and autobiographies. However, in genealogical research one is concerned only with the pedigree charts and family group records.

There are many different forms and charts available for use in genealogical research, and no specific form is required except when a family group record is submitted to The Genealogical Society for processing or filing. However, members of the L.D.S. Church should become familiar with the standard forms as printed by The Genealogical Society and learn to use them. When hiring a professional researcher or when publishing data for a family organization, use of the standard form is advised.

THE PEDIGREE CHART

The pedigree chart published by The Genealogical Society is a five-generation chart 8½ x 14 inches.

Figure 12. Pedigree Chart.

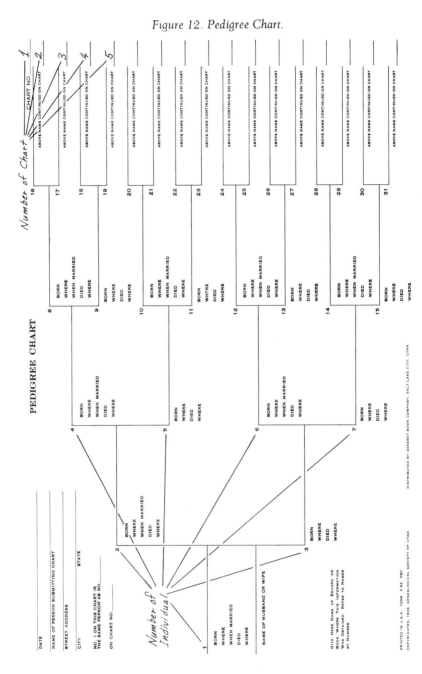

This chart provides for the listing of information of birth, marriage, and death for four generations of direct ancestry. The fifth generation is listed by name only, and each fifth generation name is *repeated* as the first generation on subseqeunt charts. Space is also provided for the name and address of the compiler as well as the current date. If the sources of information cannot be given in detail in the space provided, it is suggested that additional sources be recorded on the back of the pedigree chart.

There are two sets of reference numbers on each pedigree chart, one for individuals and one for charts.

Individuals named on the pedigree charts are referred to as person #...., on chart no. ..... The number of the individual has meaning only when the number of the chart is given; otherwise, one must read each name on the pedigree to find the individual.

Numbering Names of Individuals: Name #1 on any chart can be either a male or female. Thereafter, males (fathers) are recorded on the top, or even numbered lines, and females (mothers) on the bottom, or odd numbered lines. The numbering of individuals is most easily understood when one initiates his own pedigree chart with himself as #1.

Numbering Pedigree Charts: There are many plans for numbering pedigree charts. In some plans only numerals are used; some, letters of the alphabet; and others, a combination of both numerals and letters. The following plans are offered as suggestions, and each individual should use the plan best suited to his needs, adopting and adapting as necessary.

Plan I. Pedigree chart no. 1 is the chart upon which the individual records his own name on line #1. When it becomes necessary to extend the pedigree chart beyond chart no. 1, the blanks on the right-hand side of chart no. 1 are completed by placing the numeral "2" directly below no. 1 and continuing through no. 17. After chart no. 17, the extension is made in a systematic manner.

Figure 13.

PLAN I.

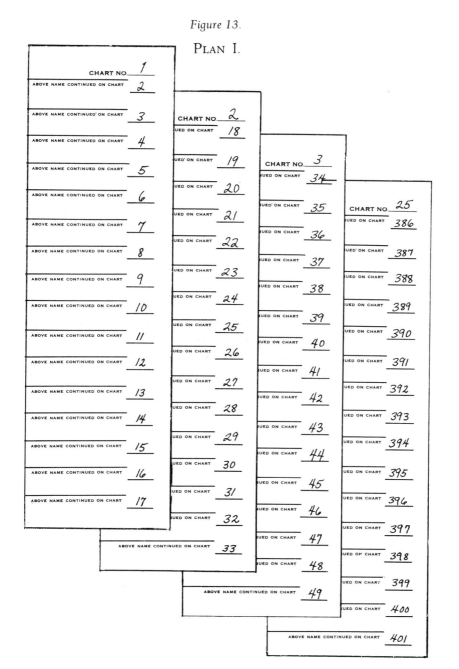

Plan II. The extension of pedigree chart no. 1 is accomplished by numbering charts no. 2 through 17. When any one of the charts numbered 2 through 17 is extended, it is done by recording on a blank pedigree chart the next consecutive number, which in this case is no. 18. When an extension is needed for another chart, whether it is one of the charts no. 2 through 17, or chart no. 18, the new chart is given the next consecutive number, 19, then 20, etc.

Figure 14.

Plan II.

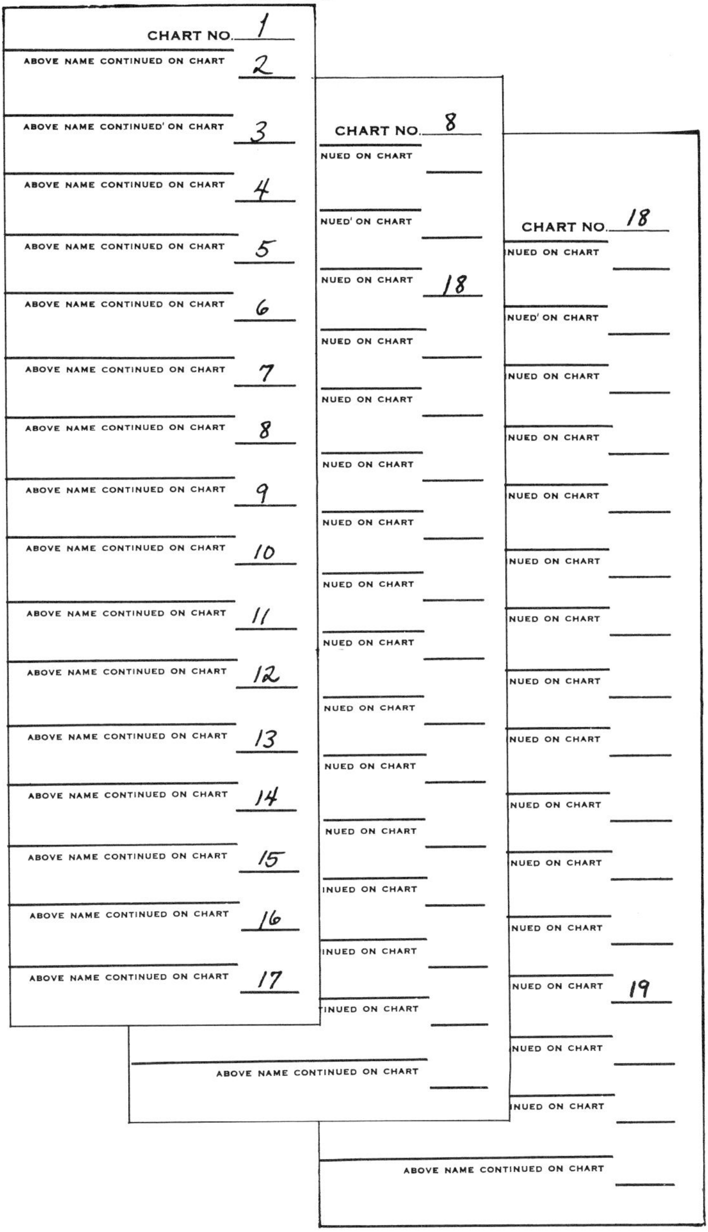

CHART NO. *1*

ABOVE NAME CONTINUED ON CHART *2*

ABOVE NAME CONTINUED' ON CHART *3*

ABOVE NAME CONTINUED ON CHART *4*

ABOVE NAME CONTINUED ON CHART *5*

ABOVE NAME CONTINUED ON CHART *6*

ABOVE NAME CONTINUED ON CHART *7*

ABOVE NAME CONTINUED ON CHART *8*

ABOVE NAME CONTINUED ON CHART *9*

ABOVE NAME CONTINUED ON CHART *10*

ABOVE NAME CONTINUED ON CHART *11*

ABOVE NAME CONTINUED ON CHART *12*

ABOVE NAME CONTINUED ON CHART *13*

ABOVE NAME CONTINUED ON CHART *14*

ABOVE NAME CONTINUED ON CHART *15*

ABOVE NAME CONTINUED ON CHART *16*

ABOVE NAME CONTINUED ON CHART *17*

ABOVE NAME CONTINUED ON CHART

CHART NO. *8*

NUED ON CHART

NUED' ON CHART

NUED ON CHART *18*

NUED ON CHART

NUED ON CHART

NUED ON CHART

NUED ON CHART

NUED ON CHART

NUED ON CHART

NUED ON CHART

NUED ON CHART

NUED ON CHART

INUED ON CHART

INUED ON CHART

TINUED ON CHART

CHART NO. *18*

NUED ON CHART

NUED' ON CHART

NUED ON CHART

NUED ON CHART

NUED ON CHART

NUED ON CHART

NUED ON CHART

NUED ON CHART

NUED ON CHART

NUED ON CHART

NUED ON CHART *19*

NUED ON CHART

INUED ON CHART

ABOVE NAME CONTINUED ON CHART

Plan III. Letters of the alphabet are substituted for numerals. Many different combinations are possible; one is shown below:

FUNDAMENTALS OF GENEALOGICAL RESEARCH

Figure 15.

PLAN III.

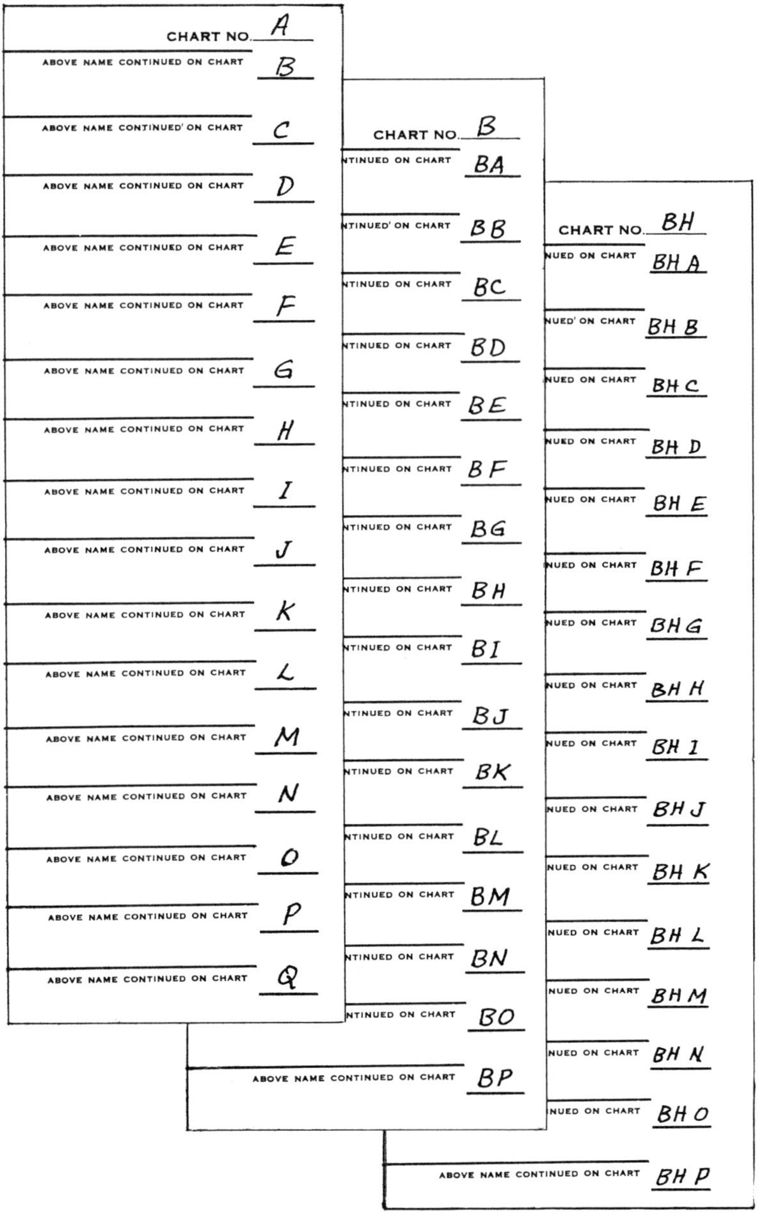

Plan IV. In this plan a combination of numerals and letters of the alphabet is used. The first seventeen charts are numbered 1 through 17, and the charts are extended by using a letter of the alphabet as well as a numeral.

Figure 16.

Plan IV.

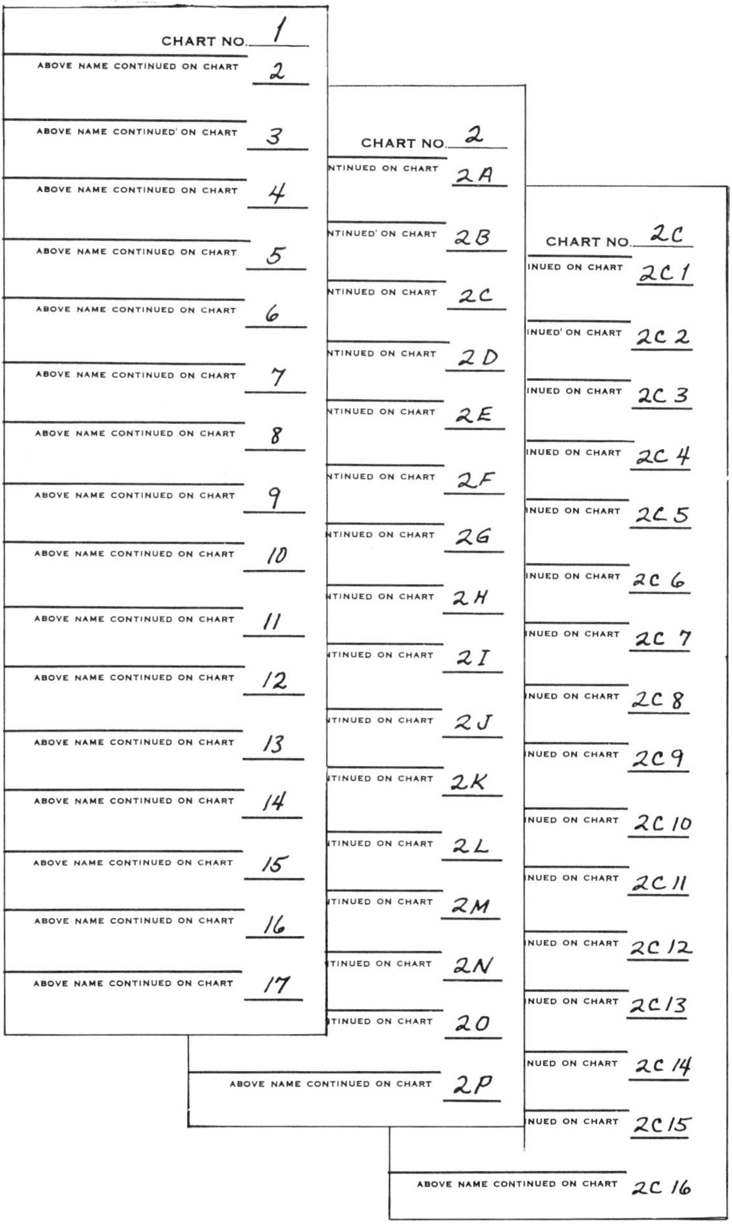

CHART NO. 1

ABOVE NAME CONTINUED ON CHART 2

ABOVE NAME CONTINUED ON CHART 3

ABOVE NAME CONTINUED ON CHART 4

ABOVE NAME CONTINUED ON CHART 5

ABOVE NAME CONTINUED ON CHART 6

ABOVE NAME CONTINUED ON CHART 7

ABOVE NAME CONTINUED ON CHART 8

ABOVE NAME CONTINUED ON CHART 9

ABOVE NAME CONTINUED ON CHART 10

ABOVE NAME CONTINUED ON CHART 11

ABOVE NAME CONTINUED ON CHART 12

ABOVE NAME CONTINUED ON CHART 13

ABOVE NAME CONTINUED ON CHART 14

ABOVE NAME CONTINUED ON CHART 15

ABOVE NAME CONTINUED ON CHART 16

ABOVE NAME CONTINUED ON CHART 17

CHART NO. 2

NTINUED ON CHART 2A

NTINUED ON CHART 2B

NTINUED ON CHART 2C

NTINUED ON CHART 2D

NTINUED ON CHART 2E

NTINUED ON CHART 2F

NTINUED ON CHART 2G

NTINUED ON CHART 2H

NTINUED ON CHART 2I

NTINUED ON CHART 2J

NTINUED ON CHART 2K

NTINUED ON CHART 2L

NTINUED ON CHART 2M

NTINUED ON CHART 2N

NTINUED ON CHART 2O

ABOVE NAME CONTINUED ON CHART 2P

CHART NO. 2C

INUED ON CHART 2C1

INUED ON CHART 2C2

INUED ON CHART 2C3

INUED ON CHART 2C4

INUED ON CHART 2C5

INUED ON CHART 2C6

INUED ON CHART 2C7

INUED ON CHART 2C8

INUED ON CHART 2C9

INUED ON CHART 2C10

INUED ON CHART 2C11

INUED ON CHART 2C12

INUED ON CHART 2C13

INUED ON CHART 2C14

INUED ON CHART 2C15

ABOVE NAME CONTINUED ON CHART 2C16

THE FAMILY RECORD BOOK 47

Cross Referencing Pedigree Charts: When a pedigree extension is made, the fifth generation name (numbers 16 through 31) is repeated on the new chart on line #1. A space is provided for cross referencing.

Figure 17.

CROSS REFERENCING PEDIGREE CHARTS

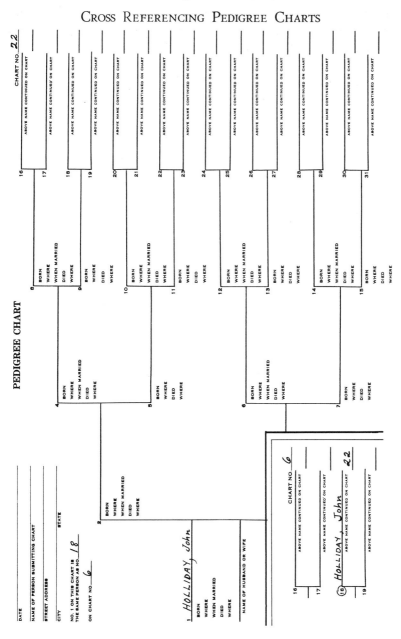

Pedigree Index: Pedigree charts should be indexed by grouping each name or surname in alphabetical order showing the chart number(s) on which the name or surname appears, as it is impossible to number the pedigree charts so that all charts containing like surnames are numbered consecutively (or located together). It is wise to leave space for future additions. The pedigree index is filed just before the no. 1 pedigree chart.

Abbott, Mary Ann, 1.
    Thomas, 8.
    William, 1, 8.
Allibone, Charlotte, 1, 9.
    Joseph, 9.
Burgess, Ruth, 27.
    Thomas, 27.
Duncan, George, 2, 18.
    Gloria, 1.
    Homer, 1.
    John, 1, 2.
    William, 2.

Oliver, John, 22.
    Thomas, 22, 39.
Powers, Rebecca, 3.
Sundman, Magdalena, 1, 17.
Towne, John, 25.
    Rebecca, 25.
    William, 25.
Wiger, Anna Catharena, 1, 15.
Whipple, Elizabeth, 3.
    Joseph, 3, 23.
    Mathew, 23.

THE FAMILY GROUP RECORD

The 8½ by 14 inch family group record published by The Genealogical Society provides space for the names of three generations, as the parents of the husband and wife are listed as well as their children. (See Figure 2, page 6.)

The family group records should be arranged in alphabetical order by the name of the husband to save time and to conform to the filing system used in the Church Records Archives. It is difficult to locate a family group record filed by relationship or generation unless the pedigree of each individual is memorized. For ease in alphabetizing and in locating the family group records, it is advisable to record the name and the birth year of the husband and the name of the wife in the upper right-hand corner of the family group record.

PROJECT ASSIGNMENTS

1. Organize your pedigree charts and arrange your family group records in alphabetical order; place them in a Family Record Book.

2. Make a pedigree index.

Chapter Six

NOTEKEEPING

■ Ideally, a notekeeping system should prevent duplication of research by (1) providing a list of the records that have been searched, and (2) giving ready access to the information obtained from the records searched. If these two items are considered, then anyone, whether familiar with the research problem or not, can easily examine the notes and learn which records have been searched, and what information was or was not found in these records.

There is no "sure" system that can be used in all circumstances and for all geographic localities. Some researchers insist that all information be extracted onto family group records and pedigree charts, forgetting that genealogical sources contain more information than is required to complete a family group form. Also, until one is certain of relationships, it is unwise to assume relationships by placing names on family group records and pedigree charts. Other researchers insist that all notes be recorded on the back of the family group record, forgetting that the back of the family group record may be too small to hold all notes, or that the information on the front may become crossed-out and scratched-over, necessitating the recopying of both the front and the back of the family group record. Still other researchers organize genealogical data into notebooks by locality, forgetting that records of one family may be in several localities or that one locality may contain records of several families and that locality names and boundaries are constantly changing.

A successful notekeeping system could include each of these ideas under certain conditions, but must be flexible enough to disregard them when practical application proves them unworkable. The following system is suggested as a guide, and the researcher should use his ingenuity in adapting or adopting that which best suits his needs. The professional researcher has different filing needs than the family researcher. Some research problems can be solved locally, while research in certain localities requires much correspondence. These conditions should be considered in establishing a workable notekeeping system.

RESEARCH FOLDER

After the genealogical researcher has organized his family group records and pedigree charts in The Family Record Book and has selected the family group record he wishes to verify, complete, and correct, he removes or copies the family group record from The Family Record Book. A portion of the pedigree applicable to the chosen family group record is also copied, and both the family group record and the pedigree are placed in the research folder. It is suggested that a manila folder be used for the survey phase, and as the problem develops into the research phase with many abstracts, extracts, certificates, etc., the material could be transferred to a ring binder.

One copy of the family group record in the research folder should always be kept current (up-to-date) and is known as the "status" family group record. It is well to file this status family group record in the front of the research folder. Family group records containing incorrect information should be destroyed. Often it is desirable to compile information from a specific source and record it on a family group record. The family group record should be documented as to the specific source and filed in the research folder for ease in analyzing and evaluating.

CALENDAR OF SEARCH

The record sources to be searched in the survey phase should be listed on calendars. A calendar is a list, grouping, or systematic arrangement of items to be searched. Calendars can be made on special forms or ruled on plain sheets of notepaper and filed in the research folder.

Researcher's Name and Address: This information should be entered on the calendar and also on all research notes to avoid loss of material. If information is worth recording, it is worth identifying.

Surnames: All surnames pertaining to the research objective should be entered on the calendar. It saves time to search for several related surnames in a jurisdiction and to extract all entries of these surnames.

Record Category or Jurisdiction: A calendar should be made for each record category or jurisdiction. The survey phase includes a calendar for the home jurisdiction, printed secondary records, and for the L.D.S. Church jurisdiction.

Library and Call Number: The name of the library and the call number should be recorded.

Source Description: The source should be briefly, but carefully, identified on the calendar with the name of the record source and the time period covered. If there is space, full bibliographic data can be included.

Date Searched: The date of search is particularly helpful to the professional researcher in writing reports and is also valuable as a reference for all researchers.

Figure 18. Calendar of Search.

	CALENDAR OF SEARCH		
RESEARCHER'S NAME AND ADDRESS: Karen Hardman, 286 Allen Blvd., Thatcher, Ariz.			
SURNAMES: Tarbet, Watterson			
RECORD CATEGORY OR JURISDICTION: L. D. S. Church			

LIBRARY AND CALL NUMBER	SOURCE DESCRIPTION	DATE SEARCHED	EXTRACT NUMBER
—	TIB	16 Nov. 1965	1
—	Finished Section family groups	4 Jan. 1966	7
—	Unfinished Section family groups	4 Jan 1966	8
—	Sealing Section family groups	4 Jan 1966	9
—	Patrons Section 1962— family group	4 Jan 1966	10
#22690 pts. 722 & 787	Patrons Section 1924-1962 groups	20 Jan 1966	16
	Card-indexed pedigrees		
#35619 Pts. 33 & 35	Alphabetized pedigrees	20 Jan 1966	17
—	Surname card index	4 Jan 1966	11
—	Early Church Information	4 Jan 1966	12
—	Marriage License Card Index	4 Jan 1966	13
#42088 pts. 33 & 35	Obituary card index	6 Dec 1965	4
#38335 pt. 12	Utah Immigration card index	18 Feb 1966	20
#38335 pts 8 & 9	European Emigration card index	18 Feb 1966	21
	Membership Card Index		

Extract Number: The extract numbers on the calendars are not necessarily in consecutive order, but refer to consecutive numbers in the research notebook. For this reason the calendar becomes an index to the research notebook.

CALENDAR OF CORRESPONDENCE

The calendar of correspondence is similar to the calendar of search. The "library and call number" column is replaced by "date reply received." It may be advisable to include more than one jurisdiction on a calendar.

Figure 19. Calendar of Correspondence.

CALENDAR OF CORRESPONDENCE			
RESEARCHER'S NAME AND ADDRESS: Karen Hardman, 286 Allen Blvd., Thatcher, Ariz.			
SURNAMES: Tarbet, Watterson			
RECORD CATEGORY OR JURISDICTION: Home and L.D.S. Church			
DATE LETTER SENT	SOURCE DESCRIPTION	DATE REPLY RECEIVED	EXTRACT NUMBER
2 Jan. 1966	Mrs. Gertrude Smalley, 266 East 400 South, Provo, Utah. $10.00 TIB Search		
16 Jan. 1966	Mark Tarbet, 255 Redwood, San Diego, Calif. Does he have Grandpa Tarbet's Bible?	30 Jan. 1966	19

Date Letter Sent: This date is the same as that on the heading of the letter and indicates the letter has been written and mailed.

Source Description: The source description includes the name and address of the person to whom the letter is being sent, a notation as to the amount of money enclosed, and the purpose of the letter.

Date Reply Received: A date in this column indicates a reply has been received. (Periodically the researcher should scan this column to see which letters are unanswered and issue follow-up letters.)

Extract Number: The extract number refers to the carbon copy of the letter sent, which copy is given a number and filed in the research folder. (Replies to letters are filed next to the copy of the letter sent.)

Calendars are used as tentative lists of sources to be searched, and some items are recorded on the calendars before visiting the library; others are recorded directly from the card catalogue. At the end of a day the researcher can quickly tell what has been searched, where the information is located in the research notebook, and what sources are yet to be searched. At the end of a year the researcher will still know what has been searched and where it is located; and, at the end of a lifetime, when someone else continues the research, this person can also tell what has been done, why, and with what results.

RESEARCH NOTEBOOK

The research notebook is a collection of research notes. For convenience, the pages of this notebook should be uniform in size. The regular 8½ by 11 inch ruled notebook paper is adequate, and the researcher can easily add vertical lines to provide columns when necessary.

Some persons prefer to use loose paper with a clip board, others like spiral binders or ring binders. The researcher should use what is best suited to his needs. Eventually the research notes could be filed in a ring type binder for preservation and for easier accessibility, or, if there is an adequate left-hand margin, the manuscript could be permanently bound.

As the records listed on the calendars are searched the information is recorded in the research notebook. The notebook entries are recorded in chronological order of search, and each entry is given an extract number in numerical order.

There are many calendars, but only one research notebook. The notebook includes information on all record categories and jurisdictions and all surnames searched. The calendar is limited to a specific record category or jurisdiction and to specific surnames.

Figure 20. Research Notes.

Research Notes—Karen Hardman, 286 Allen Blvd., Thatcher, Arizona.

1. 16 Nov. 1965—TIB. Checked Tarbet and Watterson. See folder for William Tarbet.

2. 16 Nov. 1965—Early Church Information Card Index. Searched for Fielding and Hardy. No Hardy found.
Joshua Fielding
b. 20 Apr 1837, Lancashire, Eng.
father: James Fielding
mother: Ann
Ref: Glenwood Ward, Sevier Stake, Record 1, p. 1.

3. 20 Nov. 1965—Portsmouth Branch Records, London Conference 1844 (Gen. Soc. #13656, pt. 54). No Burton or Kearl. Records very sketchy; appear to be incomplete.

4. 6 Dec. 1965—Obituary Card Index (Gen. Soc. #42088, pts. 33 & 35). No George Tarbet or Helen Watterson.

5. 6 Dec. 1965—Research Dept., Genealogical Society. Research folder for Pearl Fielding, client or patron. Collection of genealogical and historical data gathered by John Owens, researcher. Some Fielding, Henthorn, Duffin, Stott data. Many parish register extracts. Suggest to Duffin Family Organization get permission from Pearl Fielding or heirs to obtain folder from Research Department.

The date of search should be recorded in the research notebook by each extract or abstract, as well as complete bibliographic data, name of library, call number, etc. The research notebook should include comments on the condition of the record and indicate whether microfilming was poor or if pages were missing. Notations on what was not found should also be recorded along with any decisions or assumptions made.

Information extracted from record sources should be recorded exactly as found, i.e., care should be taken not to change the spelling of names or words, as no interpretation should be made at this time.

Paper is relatively inexpensive in comparison to the value of one's time; writing on only one side of the sheet is a convenience in analyzing. It is well to make carbon copies of all research notes so that the copy can be placed in the research folder. The professional researcher can conveniently send a carbon copy to his client as part of the written research report.

After all searches have been made in both the survey phase and research phase and the evidence analyzed and evaluated, an accurate copy of the family group record is kept in the research folder for future reference, and a copy is submitted to The Genealogical Society for processing. After the family group record is processed, it is returned to the compiler and copies made for distribution among members of the family organization.

Figure 21. Systematic Notekeeping.

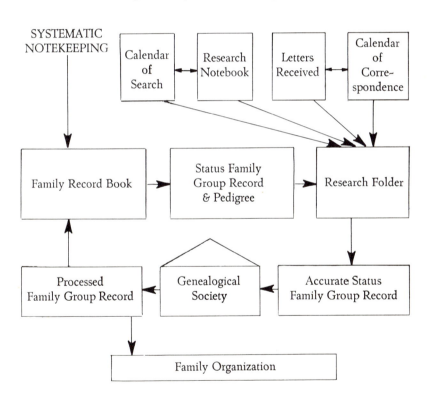

PROJECT ASSIGNMENT

1. Begin the survey phase of research by selecting one family group record from among the four generations of family group records initiated in Chapter 1. If possible, select an L.D.S. family. Initiate three calendars of search:

a. Home Jurisdiction.

b. Printed Secondary Records.

c. L.D.S. Church Jurisdiction.

Chapter Seven

FAMILY ORGANIZATION

■ A family organization is a research tool since its members provide assistance to the genealogical program of the family and help accomplish the following objectives:

1. Combine research talent and money.

2. Prevent duplication of research.

3. Extend the pedigree of the common ancestral couple and complete a family group record for each couple on the pedigree.

4. Complete a family group record for each married descendant.

5. Participate as a family in temple work to complete all ordinances for each ancestor and each descendant.

6. Disseminate information in pedigree and family group form and publish family histories.

7. Hold annual reunions to which all family members are invited.

SELECTING A COMMON ANCESTRAL COUPLE

The first step in organizing a family is to select an ancestral couple whose descendants may become members of the organization. If deceased, or because of age, the couple is unable to call their descendants together and organize the family, other family members act in their stead, selecting those best qualified for leadership, rather than following the patriarchal order.

Some suggestions for selecting the common ancestral couple follow:

1. The first couple to immigrate to the United States.

2. The first couple to settle in the locality of interest or to migrate to the West.

3. The first couple to join The Church of Jesus Christ of Latter-day Saints.

Other ideas should be considered; however, it is best to select a couple born after 1800 or the task of contacting and organizing descendants could be most difficult. Selecting a couple born much earlier would require genealogical research on the part of the descendants to prove their eligibility for membership.

CONTACTING FAMILY MEMBERS

Once the ancestral couple has been selected, a letter should be composed to inform the descendants of the purposes of the organization, what they must do to join, and when the first meeting will be held. The initial letter should be concise, neat, and professionally done.

As the family organization will want to gather information on the living as well as the deceased, a blank family group form to be completed by each married couple could be included in the letter. Space should be provided on the family group form for specifying the sources used, and a *self-addressed stamped envelope* should be enclosed with the letter for convenience in replying.

Figure 22. Sample Family Organization Letter.

GERALD ALDER FAMILY ORGANIZATION

For Descendants of Gerald Alder and Anna Sorenson

June, 1966

Dear Relative,

Several of the descendants of Gerald Alder are interested in forming a family organization and in compiling a family history. To insure that information about you and your family will be in this history, and also that it will be complete and accurate, please complete the enclosed forms, and return them within 10 days in the enclosd self-addressed stamped envelope.

Many family members have already contributed towards the family history, and their help certainly has been appreciated. Aunt Martha Hixon and Uncle Dan Alder have spent many years doing genealogical research on the Alder line and deserve many thanks for their efforts.

Please come to the reunion at Lakeside Park on Saturday, August 24, at 12:00 noon. Bring the entire family and your own picnic lunch. At 2:00 p.m. a business meeting will be held to bring you up to date on the genealogical research and to present plans for further organizing the family. It is suggested that the annual family dues be $2.00 per married couple, payable at the reunion, or $2.50 if paid at a later date. Those who pay dues this year will receive a printed family group sheet for Gerald Alder and his wife, Ann Sorenson.

Sincerely,
Henry S. Alder

Encls.

One of the most effective means of obtaining names and addresses of married descendants is to enclose in the initial letter a form on which is provided space for the names and addresses of brothers, sisters, and children. By using this means it is possible to increase a list of ten descendants to hundreds within a few months. Relatives can also be located through use of telephone books and directories, and by advertising in newspapers and genealogical exchange bulletins.

Each descendant should be contacted at least annually and more often if possible. If this is not done, the talents of many are soon lost to the organization, only a few members are left, and eventually the organization will fail.

SAMPLE CONSTITUTION

Each family organization needs a constitution or set of rules by which to govern its members. The following example could be used as a guide:

CONSTITUTION OF THE GERALD ALDER FAMILY ORGANIZATION

Article I — Name

The name of this organization shall be the Gerald Alder Family Organization.

Article II — Objectives

The objectives of this organization shall be as follows:

1. Keep alive in our hearts and in the hearts of our posterity our favored birthright.

2. Foster genealogical research and temple activity.

3. Prevent duplication of effort by combining research talent and financial resources.

4. Disseminate genealogical data to all family members.

5. Maintain family unity by holding an annual reunion and publishing an annual newsletter.

Article III — Membership

This organization shall be composed of the descendants of Gerald Alder and the husband or wife of any of his descendants.

Article IV — Officers and Committees

The business of this organization shall be conducted by the following officers and committees:

1. Board of Directors
2. President
3. Vice President
4. Genealogical Chairman
5. Genealogical Committee
6. Secretary
7. Treasurer
8. Historian

Article V — Selection of Officers

1. *Board of Directors*—shall be elected for a three-year term by members attending the reunion and shall include: (a) a representative from each of the six families of the sons and daughters of Gerald Alder, and (b) one representative from the general membership. The terms of office shall be rotated so that two directors shall be elected every year and each third year three directors shall be elected.

2. *President*—shall be appointed by the Board of Directors from among their membership for a two-year term.

3. *Vice President*—shall be appointed by the Board of Directors from among their membership for a two-year term.

4. *Genealogical Chairman*—shall be appointed by the Board of Directors from the general membership for a term as designated by the Board of Directors.

5. *Genealogical Committee*—shall be appointed by the Board of Directors with at least one representative from each of the six families of the sons and daughters of Gerald Alder. Term of office shall be designated by the Board of Directors.

6. *Secretary*—shall be appointed by the Board of Directors from the general membership for a term as designated by the Board of Directors.

7. *Treasurer*—shall be appointed by the Board of Directors from the general membership for a term as designated by the Board of Directors.

8. *Historian*—shall be appointed by the Board of Directors from the general membership for a term as designated by the Board of Directors.

Article VI — Duties of Officers and Committees

1. *Board of Directors*—shall conduct and be responsible for the affairs of the organization; shall have power to appoint as many committees and individuals as necessary to fill offices outlined in the constitution and to carry out the objectives of the organiza-

tion; shall assess dues; shall give the membership a report of the previous year's activities at each reunion; and shall act as a nominating committee to select incoming directors.

2. *President*—shall preside and conduct Board of Director meetings; and shall preside and conduct the annual family reunion.

3. *Vice President*—shall act in the absence of the president.

4. *Genealogical Chairman*—shall supervise all genealogical research done by committee members; shall act as Family Representative for submitting family group sheets to The Genealogical Society; and shall have authority to call genealogical committee meetings or special family genealogical meetings, the latter with permission of the Board of Directors.

5. *Genealogical Committee*—shall coordinate all genealogical research activity; shall compile family group records for each ancestral and each descendant couple; shall disseminate all information obtained through genealogical research.

6. *Secretary*—shall secure and maintain an up-to-date record of membership and those eligible for membership; shall inform the membership of all activities through an annual family newsletter.

7. *Treasurer*—shall keep and maintain a record of finances.

8. *Historian*—shall be responsible for a history of the organiaztion; shall cooperate with the genealogical committee in compiling family histories for publication; and shall be responsible for obtaining a history of each ancestor and each descendant.

Article VII — Amendments

This constitution may be amended at any announced reunion by a two-thirds vote of the members present.

— — — — —

It is important that the constitution be flexible to provide for the continued growth of the family, and be brief to provide for ease in interpretation and enforcement. A lengthy discussion of the constitution should be avoided at the reunion; instead, those assisting in the initial organization should prepare beforehand a constitution they feel is suitable and present it for approval.

GENEALOGICAL RESEARCH

As the organization grows it may become necessary to hold special genealogical meetings in conjunction with, or separate from, the annual reunion. These meetings could be training sessions in genealogical research where specific assignments are made to committee members.

Members of a family organization would be wise in expending a portion of their funds to train family members as research specialists. The Genealogical Chairman (family representative) should continually increase his knowledge of proper techniques and available sources. Any money invested by the family in educating its own members towards this goal would be more than repaid through the superior services rendered by these individuals to the family genealogical program.

As the pedigree is proven and complete family group records obtained, copies of the extended pedigree and family group records should be disseminated at the reunion to family members as they pay their dues. There can be no guarantee of the quantity of research information to be distributed, but each family member is entitled to a guarantee of the quality of the research.

The pedigree lines of the common ancestral couple will eventually join those of other active family organizations. A decision should be made by the Board of Directors concerning the pro-rating of funds for work on collateral lines or in combining with other families who may eventually be interested in the same pedigrees.

One family organization will not solve all research problems. Each person is a member of many families and may join more than one organization. In a well organized family there is a place for each individual to use his talents, whether searching original records, writing biographies, collecting photographs, doing secretarial work, or supervising reunions.

REORGANIZING A FAMILY

The task of reorganizing an already existing family organization is more difficult than effecting a new organization. There are many family organizations in existence which are not functioning satisfactorily for several reasons:

1. Not all descendants are contacted annually.

2. Dues are too expensive, and the young couples and older couples cannot afford to join, leaving the responsibility to a few. (Donations above the set dues can be encouraged for those who can afford it.)

3. Each branch of the family is not represented on the Board of Directors.

4. Too much time is spent discussing genealogical research during the business meeting. The details of genealogical research should be discussed in genealogical committee meetings and not before the entire group.

5. Genealogical research is either neglected or some descendants do not receive a report of the research.

6. Genealogical research is of poor quality. When family group records are printed, the sources are not properly documented, and often the ordinance dates are incorrect. Also, family funds are frequently wasted by hiring unqualified researchers.

The problems seem to fall into two groups, (1) poor organization and (2) unsatisfactory genealogical research. When officers are already functioning, it may be difficult to give constructive criticism, but often the officers would welcome friendly suggestions for a better organization. Perhaps changing the date or place of the annual reunion would result in a larger attendance. If some descendants are not being contacted, then one could suggest a means of doing it and volunteer to help with the project. Whenever criticism is offered, it is well to give the reasons for the criticism and then suggest ways to correct the problem.

The problem of unsatisfactory genealogical research can be solved when those skilled in genealogical research are appointed to the Genealogical Committee. Those who show interest in genealogical research are frequently the ones who are appointed to do the family research. However, often those who show interest are not skilled or experienced, and those who may be well qualified are not always known to the officers of the family organization. Those with special genealogical skill should make themselves known to the family, and the best way to do this is by showing the results of their research. One might prepare accurate family group records and take them to the reunion to be displayed where relatives could view his work and copy information. Family members soon find it impossible to copy all they would like, and this offers an opportunity for suggestions concerning the family organization's research problems.

SUGGESTED READING

The Genealogical Society of The Church of Jesus Christ of Latter-day Saints, Inc. *Genealogical Instruction Manual, Family Organizations, Supplement C.* Salt Lake City: 1966.

Chapter Eight

LIBRARIES

■ Libraries, as a repository of source material, are aids to the genealogical researcher. Libraries keep records of past events, store knowledge for future use, and are of various types: civic, school or university, hospital, business firm, law firm, newspaper, and home. Regardless of the type of library, in each can be found information of use to the genealogical researcher.

Libraries are not the place to begin genealogical research, nor are they a learning device for beginning researchers, but the success one has at a library depends upon (1) his genealogical training, (2) his knowledge of libraries, (3) the collection of the library, and (4) the librarian's genealogical training. One cannot expect library employees to analyze pedigrees as their responsibility is to make available to the patron the records on deposit.

CARD CATALOGUE

The key or index to the holdings of a particular library is the card catalogue and it is consulted first. It is sometimes referred to as a dictionary-type catalogue because the cards are arranged alphabetically. Cards are made for each book or record, but, generally the parts of books, magazines, etc., are not indexed in the card catalogue. Usually there are at least three cards in the catalogue representing each book or record:

1. An author card.

2. A title card.

3. One or more subject cards.

The card catalogue is an aid in surveying the library holdings on a particular subject. In most libraries a locality is catalogued as a subject. When one does not know the exact title or author's name, the subject is the logical beginning approach.

The following are examples of cards from the card catalogue with an analysis of the information available to the patron through this means:

Figure 23. Author Card.

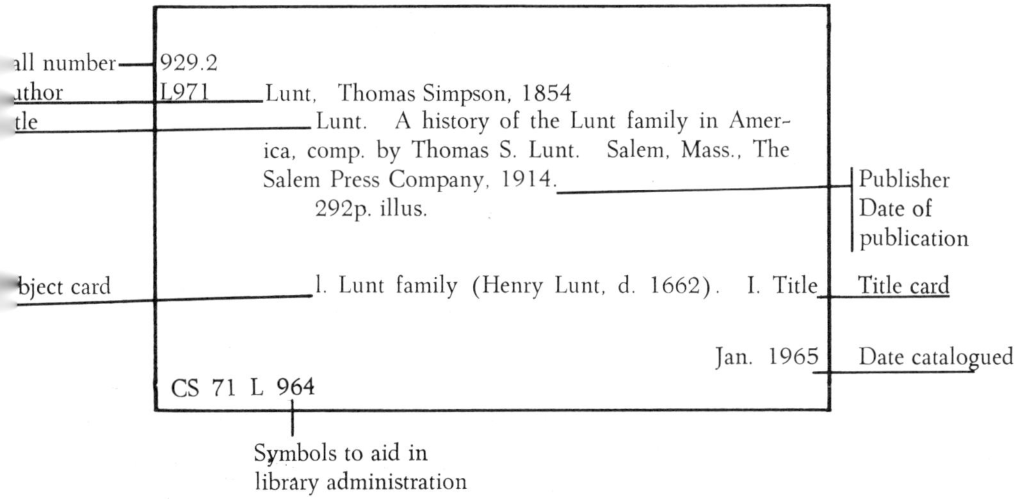

all number —— 929.2
uthor   L971   Lunt, Thomas Simpson, 1854
tle   Lunt.   A history of the Lunt family in America, comp. by Thomas S. Lunt.   Salem, Mass., The Salem Press Company, 1914._____ Publisher
                              292p. illus.   Date of publication

bject card   1. Lunt family (Henry Lunt, d. 1662). I. Title Title card

                                                      Jan. 1965 Date catalogued
              CS 71 L 964

Symbols to aid in
library administration

Figure 24. Title Card.

```
            LUNT
929.2
L971    Lunt,  Thomas Simpson, 1854
            Lunt.  A history of the Lunt family in Amer-
        ica, comp. by Thomas S. Lunt.  Salem, Mass., The
        Salem Press Company, 1914.
            292p. illus.


            1. Lunt family (Henry Lunt, d. 1662).  I. Title


                                            Jan.  1965
```

Figure 25. Subject Card.

```
929.2       LUNT FAMILY (HENRY LUNT, d. 1662).
L971    Lunt,  Thomas Simpson, 1854
            Lunt.  A history of the Lunt family in Amer-
        ica, comp. by Thomas S. Lunt.  Salem, Mass., The
        Salem Press Company, 1914.
            292p. illus.


            1. Lunt family (Henry Lunt, d. 1662).  I. Title


                                            Jan.  1965
```

Information at the bottom of the cards indicates the title and subject cards which were made for a particular book. Author, title, and subject cards are identical except for the heading at the top of the card which is added for title and subjects.

CLASSIFICATION

As records are acquired it is necessary to assign them to a specific location in the library "stacks" (library shelves). A classification system is used to shelve all books on like subjects together. The most commonly used system in the United States is the Dewey Decimal Classification. In this system books are classified by grouping them in ten main subject classes:

000	General Works	500	Pure Science
100	Philosophy	600	Applied Science
200	Religion	700	The Arts
300	Social Science	800	Literature
400	Language	900	History

The ten main subject classes can be further sub-divided into special fields. For instance, class 900-999, history, is sub-divided into nine special classes, which are further sub-divided. Genealogy is grouped under biography, 920, and assigned the number 929.

900 History
    920 Biography

921	Philosophy	926	Applied Sciences
922	Religion	927	Arts and Recreation
923	Social Science	928	Literature
924	Linguistics	929	Genealogy and Heraldry
925	Pure Sciences		

The call number for each book is composed of the classification number which denotes the subject of the book and the author, or Cutter, number which denotes the author:

929.1 — subject or classification number
Call number   (genealogy)
B24 — author or Cutter number (Bennett)

The call number for a specific book varies with each library; therefore, it is necessary to add the name of the library when recording call numbers for future reference. Note the following call numbers for the *Genealogical Instruction Manual:*

Brigham Young University Library— 929.1
G286g

Library of The Genealogical Society— Ref
929.1
G286i

There may be symbols above or in front of the call number which indicates a specific location in the library:

Ref — denotes the book will be found in the reference section.

Reg — denotes detailed information will be found in a register, probably in the reference section.

Map — denotes the record will be found with the map collection.

If there is doubt concerning symbols in the call number, the librarian should be consulted.

LIBRARY DEPARTMENTS

There are different departments in libraries depending upon their size and type. A library may contain any of the following departments and services:

Reading Room: Each library has a reading room equipped with desks or tables for study purposes.

Circulation or Loan Department: In this department one may "check-out" books and learn the regulations governing the library. If the library has "open stacks," the borrower finds the book he wants and checks it out at the loan desk. If it has "closed stacks," the borrower presents a call slip properly filled out, and an attendant will find the book. Some special libraries do not allow their books to circulate (be checked out); in this case there is no circulation or loan department.

Reserve Book Room: If a large number of persons must use a small number of books, or a specific book is assigned to all class members, it is sometimes necessary to place the book or books on reserve so all can have an equal opportunity to use the assigned books. Reserve books are often loaned for varying periods, and the reserve librarians help with the regulations governing this department.

Reference Department: In most libraries there are books which are consulted frequently for specific kinds of information. These books are not allowed to circulate and are arranged in one central location called the reference room or reference library. Any book may be used as a reference book, but more specifically the term refers to encyclopedias, dictionaries, directories, gazetteers, bibliographies, indexes, almanacs, etc. Reference librarians are trained and willing to help when specific information is needed and can give assistance at the card catalogue.

Periodical Department: A periodical or magazine is a publication which is issued at regular intervals. The current periodicals and indexes are often located in a special department; older volumes are often bound and located in the stacks.

Government Documents: Publications issued by governments are not always catalogued because of the space required. If a library has a separate department for documents, the attendant can give assistance in locating information.

Microfilm Room: Microfilm is used to conserve space and to reproduce old, worn, or rare publications for more general use. In many libraries a special room is devoted to microfilm and microfilm reading machines.

Browsing Room: Larger, modern libraries often have browsing rooms where one may relax with a variety of books at his disposal.

Music Room: Special rooms are often provided for a collection of musical scores and records. These rooms usually have their own index or card catalogue.

Map Collection: Maps are often organized in special areas because of their nature and varying size.

Departmental Libraries: It is not unusual in universities to find special libraries located in buildings other than the main library building, such as a business library, biological science library, or fine arts library. The books in these libraries are represented by cards in the main catalogue; but, often the only copy will be in the departmental libraries in other buildings.

Inter-library Loan: A valuable service to the genealogical researcher is the inter-library loan which consists of borrowing library materials from one library for the use of patrons of another library. Libraries will not loan materials to patrons who live outside their specific geographic area of circulation; but, the libraries of which they are patrons can borrow books from other libraries. Attendants at the circulation desk can inform one if such a service is available.

Surname Index: Some libraries, particularly genealogical libraries and historical societies, have a surname index which contains index cards about individuals listed in periodicals, histories, biographies, etc. This is information which is not easily located through the card catalogue.

Vertical File: The vertical file provides information on topics of current interest. Pamphlets, newspaper clippings, and pictures are often filed in large folders or envelopes and arranged alphabetically by subject. The librarian obtains information from this file for the library patron.

Special Collections: Some libraries specialize in collecting information of particular interest to their patrons, and it is organized into a special collections area.

Copying Service: Many libraries have a department where certain library materials can be reproduced for the patron. A variety of processes are available for making these reproductions, and they vary with each library as does the cost of the service.

Services and records available in libraries differ as do the rules that govern the libraries. When in doubt, one should never hesitate to inquire of the librarians as they are happy to assist. Simple questions concerning services available to patrons via correspondence or general information about libraries can often be answered by writing directly to a library. The majority of libraries are not equipped to answer large volumes of mail, nor do they undertake genealogical research for patrons; but, they often recommend persons to undertake searches in their records. Libraries are established to serve the patrons; one should learn of these services and use them wisely.

SUGGESTED READING

Knight, Hattie M. *The 1-2-3 Guide to Libraries.* rev. ed. Provo, Utah: Brigham Young University Press, 1964.

SECTION III

THE SURVEY PHASE OF GENEALOGICAL RESEARCH

Chapter Nine

BEGINNING THE SURVEY PHASE

■ A review of previous research in genealogy is a prerequisite to original research.

1. One saves both time and expense by surveying and collecting what has been done by others.

2. One becomes aware that previous research is not always accurate and complete.

3. A beginning genealogical researcher can compare and sometimes verify his research by reviewing research performed by others.

4. One becomes acquainted with the record sources in the survey as to content, time period, availability, genealogical application, and genealogical limitations.

5. One will undoubtedly discover information which has been lost to the family for several generations.

The objective of the survey phase in genealogical research is to lay a foundation for the research phase by extracting and organizing information from the home jurisdiction or record category, specific printed secondary records, and the L.D.S. Church jurisdiction. In the survey phase, family group records are very seldom completed; a complete and verified family group record is usually the result of both the survey phase and the research phase.

HOME JURISDICTION

The survey phase of genealogical research includes records initiated in the home (home jurisdiction), and these records are classified as the home record category. One begins the survey phase by searching records in his own home, then proceeds to the home records of (1) immediate relatives, (2) distant relatives, and (3) old timers native to the locality.

While searching for records in the home jurisdiction one may find records from other jurisdictions and record categories, and it is well to accumulate this information. However, one is not expected to understand all of these records until he has studied the particular locality or jurisdiction from which the records originated.

The home can be compared in this respect to a historical society library which may *initiate* certain records as part of the social and commercial jurisdiction, and these records would be classified as being in the social and commercial record category. However, the historical society library could also *store* records from other categories, such as census records. The fact that these census records are stored in the library does not change their record category from census to social and commercial. This same comparison is true of many of the records found in the home.

Genealogical testimony from the home jurisdiction is either oral or documentary (original or copied); the source of this testimony is either primary or secondary. The form in which this testimony is found can vary from a spoken word to a written word, from a scrap of brown paper to a published volume. The following are representative of testimony from the home jurisdiction:

Tradition: Oral testimony in the home which has been passed verbally from one generation to another is called tradition. Traditions are not always true, but often contain elements of truth which lead to primary sources.

Family Bible Records: Genealogical information found in Bibles usually concerns births, marriages, and deaths and is most often located on the pages between the Old and New Testaments. It is not always possible to determine whether this information is from a primary or secondary source. When examining a family Bible record, it is important to note whether or not the Bible was published before or after the dates of the recorded events. If the events occurred before the publication date, then there was a time lapse between the date of the event and the date of its recording.

It is also important to note whether all entries are written in the same handwriting and with the same pencil or ink. If it appears that several entries were recorded at the same time, then it is possible that there was a time lapse between the date of the event and the date of its recording.

The address of the publisher or any other addresses may be clues to places of residence.

Diaries and Journals: Genealogical information from diaries and journals is especially valuable as the information was often recorded at or near the time of the event, and the informant or recorder was often a witness or a participant to the recorded events, resulting in information from a primary source.

Photographs: Inscriptions on photographs often lead to the solution of genealogical problems, particularly concerning relationships.

Letters: Family letters tell of events at or near the time of the event, and the recorder could be closely associated with the event, resulting in information from a primary source. Items that should be particularly noted when examining family letters are (1) the name of the writer and the addressee, (2) the relationship of the writer to the addressee, (3) the address to which the letter was mailed, and (4) the date and place the letter was written or postmarked.

A genealogical problem involving members of the L.D.S. Church may require less searching in the home jurisdiction than a non-L.D.S. problem as often the genealogical data from the home jurisdiction is much the same as that found in L.D.S. Church records, and it is often easier to go directly to the records of the L.D.S. Church. Contemporary non-L.D.S. problems are not easily solved through L.D.S. Church records, and it is important in these problems that the home jurisdiction be thoroughly searched to lay a proper foundation for the remainder of the survey phase and the research phase.

PRINTED SECONDARY RECORDS

After reviewing the records of the home jurisdiction, the second step in the survey phase is to search certain printed secondary records. The genealogical researchers can save time and expense by extracting information from previously compiled family histories and genealogies. Though errors may be found, records of this type lay a valuable foundation for searching original records and primary sources.

In searching for printed family histories and genealogies, the first step is to search card catalogues and indexes for the specific surname of the objective and progressively consider other surnames as follows:

1. Full name of the objective.
2. Surname of the objective in general.
3. Maiden surname of the mother.
4. Surname of the spouse.
5. Maiden surname of the mother-in-law.
6. Surnames and maiden surnames of the children's spouses.

The type of surname is often a determining factor in the way a researcher attempts to solve a genealogical problem. In considering the surname approach for locating a family history, a common surname such as Adams is represented by hundreds of family histories and the search should be restricted to a specific full name in a small area. There usually would not be as many published family histories or genealogies for an uncommon surname, and a search in the indexes or card catalogue for these would be less time-consuming. The patronymic surname that changes with each generation would involve searching for the full name of the individual. A search by surname only is not recommended.

Printed secondary records such as maps, atlases, and gazetteers are also of value in the survey phase as they aid in properly identifying place names and establishing localities for use in the research phase.

PROJECT ASSIGNMENTS

1. Search the home jurisdiction for information on the family group problem selected in Chapter 6.

2. Check the card catalogue at local libraries for printed family histories and genealogies about your family.

Chapter Ten

ORGANIZATION OF THE CHURCH OF JESUS CHRIST OF LATTER-DAY SAINTS

■ The affairs of The Church of Jesus Christ of Latter-day Saints are administered by members who hold the Priesthood. The President of The Church and his counselors are Presiding High Priests and are referred to as the First Presidency. The First Presidency has authority over all the affairs pertaining to The Church as a whole, and is assisted by the Council of the Twelve Apostles. There are Assistants to the Council of the Twelve Apostles. There is a First Council of the Seventy consisting of seven men who preside over the Quorums of the Seventy (70 persons per quorum including 7 presidents). There are also Quorums of Elders (96 per quorum), Priests (48 per quorum), Teachers (24 per quorum), and Deacons (12 per quorum). There are also Quorums of High Priests, and there are Evangelists or Patriarchs.

GEOGRAPHIC DIVISIONS
   The Church of Jesus Christ of Latter-day Saints functions through geographic divisions:

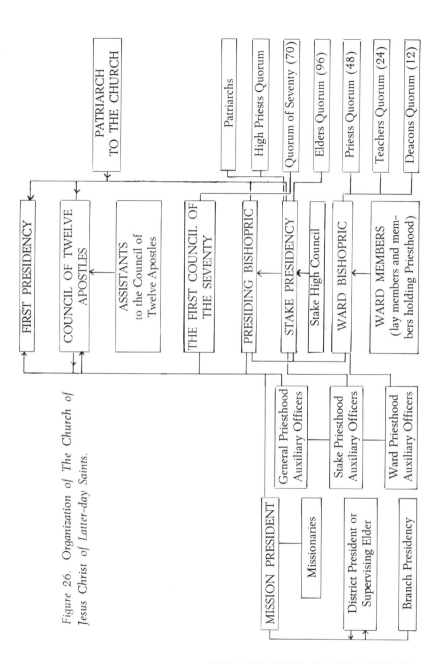

Figure 26. Organization of The Church of Jesus Christ of Latter-day Saints.

Stake: The Church, outside the mission field, is divided geographically into stakes. A stake is usually organized when a sufficient number of Latter-day Saints (3,000 to 4,000) have gathered in a locality.

Ward: Each stake is divided into wards of usually 400 to 500 memberships.

Independent Branch: Occasionally an independent branch is formed within a stake when there is an insufficient number of members to function as a ward.

Dependent Branch: A group of members too small to form a ward or independent branch may be organized as a dependent branch, dependent upon and, in part, supervised by the nearest ward or independent branch.

Mission: The mission organization corresponds in part with stake organizations; however, membership is usually relatively small and widely scattered. The mission is divided into districts (formerly called conferences) for convenience in administration, and the districts are divided into branches, which correspond to wards. When membership increases, the mission or part of it may become a stake, and the branches or some of them become wards.

ADMINISTRATIVE AUTHORITIES

There are three classes of authorities and officers of The Church: (1) General, (2) Stake or Mission, and (3) Ward or Branch.

General: General Authorities and General Officers direct churchwide activities. The First Presidency directs all affairs and activities of The Church and is assisted by the Council of the Twelve Apostles. Other General authorities include Assistants to the Council of the Twelve Apostles, the First Council of the Seventy, the Patriarch to The Church, and the Presiding Bishopric. In addition there are General Officers: members of Priesthood committees, historians, presiding officers and boards of the Priesthood auxiliary organizations (Relief Society, Sunday School, Young Men's Mutual

Improvement Association, Young Women's Mutual Improvement Association, and Primary). The Church Department of Education may also be included under the heading of Priesthood auxiliary organizations. (The Genealogical Society is under the direction of a General Priesthood committee.)

Stake: A stake is presided over by a president and two counselors, all of whom are High Priests and who function under the direction of the First Presidency of The Church and The Council of the Twelve. The Stake Presidency is assisted by a Stake High Council whose members are High Priests. Members of the Stake Presidency supervise the affairs of their stake; both Priesthood and Priesthood auxiliary organizations function under their direction.

Ward: A ward is presided over by a bishop and two counselors, all of whom are High Priests. Bishops are responsible to the Stake President, and all ward officers and members are responsible to the bishop. The program of the ward organizations is supervised by members of the bishopric. These programs originate with the General Priesthood committees and Priesthood auxiliary boards.

Mission: A mission is presided over by a president, and he is often assisted by counselors. He is responsible to the First Presidency of The Church or their duly appointed representatives. The Mission President directs, and is assisted by full-time and part-time missionaries. A mission is often divided into districts (formerly called conferences) which are presided over by a district president or supervising elder who is accountable to the Mission President. A branch is presided over by a branch president who is supervised by either a district president or a mission president. A branch in a mission corresponds somewhat to a ward in a stake.

SUGGESTED READING

Widtsoe, John A. *Priesthood and Church Government in The Church of Jesus Christ of Latter-day Saints.* Salt Lake City: Deseret Book Company, 1965.

Chapter Eleven

THE GENEALOGICAL SOCIETY

■ A major portion of the survey phase is conducted in the records of The Church of Jesus Christ of Latter-day Saints and necessitates research in the record holdings of the Church Historian's Office (C.H.O.), the Presiding Bishop's Office (P.B.O.), and the library of The Genealogical Society of the Church of Jesus Christ of Latter-day Saints, Inc. (The Genealogical Society). Many records in the C.H.O. and the P.B.O. of value to the genealogical researcher are available on microfilm at the library of The Genealogical Society.

The Genealogical Society of The Church of Jesus Christ of Latter-day Saints, Inc. is governed by a Board of Trustees composed of general priesthood officers. The library is one of the departments and activities of The Genealogical Society and was established at the time The Genealogical Society of Utah was incorporated and organized in November, 1894.

The Genealogical Society of Utah "unofficially" became The Genealogical Society of The Church of Jesus Christ of Latter-day Saints about 1933-1935, and after that date, publications are found issued under both names. In November, 1944 an official re-incorporation was made and the name legally changed to The Genealogical Society of The Church of Jesus Christ of Latter-day Saints.

In 1962 another re-incorporation was effected and the articles of incorporation were altered to include the full name, The Genealogical Society of The Church of Jesus Christ of Latter-day Saints, Inc. For a brief period prior to this incorporation the name "Genealogical Association" was in use, but this was not a legal designation.

CLASSIFICATION AND CATALOGUING

Many of the holdings of the library of The Genealogical Society are records which have originated in the L.D.S. Church. However, the major part of their holdings consists of microfilm copies of original records from many parts of the world and are of interest to all persons engaged in genealogical research. Sometimes it is possible to accomplish more at this library, in less time, than in the original records of a specific locality as the records are conveniently available in one central location.

The Dewey Decimal Classification system is used at the library of The Genealogical Society, and each record is assigned a number according to its subject or locality. In most classification systems a letter and a number are placed below the Dewey number and are referred to as the Cutter, or author number. Because of the many records at the library of The Genealogical Society for which the author is unknown, or for which there are many authors, e.g., land and probate records, the library of The Genealogical Society has established what might be termed an "expansion" of the usual Cutter (author) number and assigns the author space a symbol which indicates the type of record such as the following:

D3   Biography
H2   History
M2   Military records and pensions
R2   Land and property

S2   Probate and guardianship
V2   Vital records

The card catalogue at the library of The Genealogical Society consists of a dictionary type, or alphabetical listing, of each record by subject, author, and title. A locality is catalogued as a subject, and because of the special value of locality in genealogical research, additional locality cards are made to aid the library patron.

MICROFILM

Microfilm is used to conserve space and to reproduce old, worn, or rare publications for more general use. At the library of The Genealogical Society, microfilmed records are designated by an "F" prefix and a serial number such as 4521. More than one roll of microfilm may have the same serial number (6193) and classification number (F, 289.3, C454ca), but a different part number (Pt. 1, Pt. 2, Pt. 3, etc.) is assigned to each roll of microfilm. There is no set standard for the order in which the books or records appear on each roll of microfilm. More than one book, or record type, may be reproduced on the same roll of film, or several rolls of film may be required to film one record. If the filming appears to be of poor quality, one should consider searching the original record. In the microfilming process it is possible that pages may be missed, and sometimes these missing pages or cards which are out of place will appear at the end of the microfilm roll. For records which are kept current, particularly indexes, one should be aware of the microfilming date. (It requires practice to read microfilms. The researcher will find that if he focuses his eyes on one particular spot on the screen while turning the reel, he will not become dizzy.)

BRANCH LIBRARIES

The library of The Genealogical Society was established for the purpose of collecting, compiling, and maintaining a reservoir of genealogical source material. Branch libraries have been established to make these resources available to the L.D.S. Church members living outside the Salt Lake City area. Microfilms can be borrowed from the library of The Genealogical Society for the use of branch library patrons by consulting a microfilmed copy of the main card catalogue available at branch libraries.

Branch libraries are organized under the direction of the regional Priesthood genealogy leaders. Each library is governed by a board consisting of several stake presidents with the regional genealogical chairman serving as chairman of the library board. When a branch library is organized in an isolated area, a stake president is chairman of the board with as many Priesthood leaders as needed.

Each branch library is self-supporting. It is the responsibility of the board to provide proper physical facilities consisting of at least two reading machines, film cabinets, tables, etc. Certain basic reference books should be available at the branch library.

RESEARCH ACCREDITATION

The Genealogical Society administers examinations on research in various localities and furnishes upon request a list of researchers accredited by The Genealogical Society. The examination program is open to anyone who applies and is administered on a geographic basis. It consists of a written examination in language for the non-English speaking localities, reading early handwriting of the locality, tabulation of a family group record, knowledge of L.D.S. Church record sources, and knowledge of specific record sources and research procedures for the locality. If the individual passes the written examination on these subjects, he presents to a board of examiners a pedigree problem he has successfully completed and is subject to oral examination.

The Genealogical Society does not guarantee the work of the accredited researcher, nor his honesty, but refers names of individuals who have shown a certain proficiency in research through examination. (Accredited researchers have access to the Temple Records Index Bureau. See Chapter 12.)

RESEARCH DEPARTMENT

For many years The Genealogical Society maintained a research department through which individuals or family organizations could hire genealogical research. This service of the Research Department was eliminated in 1966. The files which were assembled by this department are most valuable and should be checked to avoid duplication of research. The Research Department maintained an alphabetical card index listing the name and address of the individual hiring the research. There is no index to surnames for which research was performed.

Many accounts have been inactive for years and may not be known to the present family members. To obtain information from the files of the Research Department it is necessary to (1) learn the name of the individual or family organization who hired the Research Department, as this is the name under which the information is filed, and (2) obtain permission from the individual or family organization. The Research Department is legally obligated to retain the research files for the benefit of the client. If the client is deceased, then his heirs are legally entitled to the information in the files. "Where these files are requested the Genealogical Society will microfilm them and retain the microfilm for their own files and return all original information to the patron who requests it."[1]

PROCESSING FAMILY GROUP RECORDS

The Genealogical Society acts as a clearing house for family group records submitted for temple ordinance work. Ward record examiners (district examiners in the missions) check family group records before they are submitted to The Genealogical Society. The family group records are received at The Genealogical Society, either by mail or in person, where they are briefly checked for accuracy in compilation and labeled with the name of the family representative and patron (person submitting the record). The Genealogical Society maintains a progress record on each family group record which shows the location of the family group record during processing. Family group records are considered acceptable when the information submitted appears to meet The Genealogical Society's standards of recording and research, with all genealogical information being consistent and no conflict with records previously processed.

---

[1]Letter from President Theodore M. Burton, Vice President and Managing Director, The Genealogical Society of The Church of Jesus Christ of Latter-day Saints, Inc., Salt Lake City, June 18, 1965.

If family group records do not meet the established standards they are returned to the compiler. Family group records which meet the established standards are sent to the Temple Records Index Bureau (See Chapter 12), where they are checked for previous endowment work. Notations concerning endowment cards (Temple Records Index Bureau cards) are made in red, other notations are recorded in green. The following symbols are used:

Red notations— C   no card found, name clearned for temple work

T   card found, name presently at temple

E   card found, individual previously endowed

.   no endowment work to be done at this time

Green notations—@ indicates a family group record for an additional marriage on file in Main Records Section, Church Records Archives

_l_   individual now living or less than 110 years old, no ordinance work to be performed at this time.

★   indicates individual appears on another family group record submitted in same group

_ar_   indicates individual appears on another family group record already on file in Main Records Section, Church Records Archives.

After the family group records are checked in the Temple Records Index Bureau, they are examined to determine the extent of duplication. Some ordinance dates may be added to the records if temple work has been performed previously and if there is no question of identity. Temple Records Index Bureau cards (endowment cards) are prepared for temple work and filing, and the original family group record, with notations, is returned to the patron.

After the ordinances are performed, the family group record is filed in the Main Records Section (finished and unfinished sections) of the Church Records Archives, and a copy of the family group record is sent to the patron.

When there is conflicting information between the family group record being processed and that previously submitted, an employee of The Genealogical Society attempts to determine whether enough data has been provided to resolve the conflict; if not, the family group record is returned to the compiler or patron with instructions and suggestions for resolving the conflict.

"As a matter of administrative policy it is assumed that compilers are truthful and send in information in good faith. For this reason it is assumed that the existing record on file is correct. If errors or conflicts occur, it is the responsibility of the second compiler to furnish sufficient proof to establish his or her claim."[2]

PEDIGREE REFERRAL SERVICE

The Pedigree Referral Service (P.R.S.) is a service of The Genealogical Society designed to help individuals and family organizations with their genealogical research by bringing together persons who have common lines of ancestry so they can co-ordinate and combine their research efforts and prevent duplication of research. This is done through a central registration file at The Genealogical Society.

The program has two phases: (1) Registration—Individuals and family organizations are encouraged to register a list of the surnames on their pedigree along with the localities and time periods involved. Family organizations should register through their family representative or genealogical chairman all surnames for which that organization is responsible. Surnames appearing on an individual's pedigree which are not included in the research program of a family

---

[2]The Church of Jesus Christ of Latter-day Saints. Priesthood Genealogy Committee, *Priesthood Correlation Manual of Instruction for the Priesthood Genealogical Program* (Salt Lake City: 1964), p. 65.

organization are registered by the individual. (2) Request for Information—Individuals and family organizations pay for requested searches for the names and addresses of those who have similar lines of ancestry.

FAMILY ORGANIZATION FILE

The Genealogical Society maintains a card file which lists the names of family organizations, the date of organization, date registered, P.R.S. number, and the names and addresses of officers. This card file is available to the public.

SUGGESTED READING

The Genealogical Society of The Church of Jesus Christ of Latter-day Saints, Inc. *Genealogical Instruction Manual, Pedigree Referral Service, Supplement B.* Salt Lake City: 1965.

The Genealogical Society of The Church of Jesus Christ of Latter-day Saints, Inc. *Genealogical Instruction Manual, Ward Record Examination, Supplement.* Salt Lake City: 1965.

Stevenson, J. Grant. *Genealogical Society Rulings.* Provo, Utah: Stevenson Supply, 1962.

Chapter Twelve

TEMPLE RECORDS INDEX BUREAU

■ The Temple Records Index Bureau (T.I.B.) is the most valuable record source in the survey phase of genealogical research. For L.D.S. pedigree problems it is always the first step of the survey phase; for non-L.D.S. pedigrees it is the first step after searching the home jurisdiction. The records to search in the next step of the survey phase are determined by the information found in the T.I.B.; the order of search varies with each pedigree problem.

ORIGIN

The Temple Records Index Bureau is a Church-wide index to endowments performed for both the living and the dead and was established for the purpose of preventing duplication of temple ordinances. Endowments performed from the days of Nauvoo to the present are entered on T.I.B. cards.

The program of copying the data from the original records was initiated in 1921 and copying began in 1922. The copying task took nearly five years to complete, and the T.I.B. was first used in processing family group records in January, 1927. After 1927, cards were made as endowments were performed and the file has been kept current. Prior to 1942 the T.I.B. was a department under the Church Historian's and Recorder's Office, but on January 1, 1942 it became a department of The Genealogical Society. By July, 1940 there were 11,159,299 names which had been checked in the T.I.B. and 1,155,116 duplications had been avoided. In 1965 there were more than 29,000,000 T.I.B. cards on file.

Figure 27. T.I.B. Card.

INDEX CARD TO		TEMPLE RECORDS	
No.	No.	Book	Page
Name in full			
When born			
Where born			
When died			
Father			
Mother			
When married		to	
Instance of		Rel.	
When baptized		When Endowed	
Sealed Husband Wife		To Parents	
References			

CONTENTS

The Temple Records Index Bureau is an *index to endowments only.* No attempt has been made to index all sealing records and all baptism records. There may be baptism and sealing dates included on the T.I.B. cards, and a few cards contain information from early sealing records but *the T.I.B. does not contain a record of all sealings nor of all baptisms.*

Cards of different color and style are used to indicate information on or about a particular individual—white cards for females, buff cards for males. There are a few salmon colored cards showing early sealing information, mainly for the Endowment House and early Utah period and some early Salt Lake Temple sealings. When temple work is in process temporary pink slips are filed for female names and green slips for male names. These slips remain in the file until the ordinances are completed, at which time they are replaced with permanent cards.

All of the information on a T.I.B. card may not have been recorded at the same time. The data recorded in red is an addition and usually has been supplied by a person other than the one giving the first information. The information added in red is considered a "correction" but it cannot be considered reliable unless a reliable source for the information is established.

A "P" and/or "C" in the upper left-hand corner of a T.I.B. card indicates that the individual appears as a parent and/or child on a family group record(s) in the Main Records Section (finished and unfinished sections) of the Church Records Archives. (See Chapter 13.)

The following asterisks (*) are included on some cards for persons endowed after 1942:

*—Name was processed from an old style record where names were not listed in family group form.

**—Name does not appear on a family group record in the Main Records Section of the Church Records Archives. During the first four months in 1943, no copies of family group records were made for the Church Records Archives because there was a backlog of family group records for processing.

***—Indicates that the parents of the individual have been endowed.

"Instance of" and "heir" are terms formerly used for what is now the family representative. This person was usually the first or oldest member of a family in the L.D.S. Church, and his name was often used as heir long after his death. The family representative must be a living individual, a blood relative to the deceased, and a baptized member of the L.D.S. Church.

Many T.I.B. cards show recent proxy baptism dates with earlier endowment dates; a note on the bottom of these cards indicates a reconfirmation of the endowment. This most often pertains to early members of the L.D.S. Church who did not know, or did not give a complete baptism date at the time of endowment. When it is impossible to find the complete baptism date through ward and branch records, family records, missionary journals, etc., the individual is re-baptized by proxy. This re-baptism is performed as The Genealogical Society discovers the omission, or it can be initiated by a patron submitting a family group record.

The T.I.B. cards are filed phonetically by surname. Cards bearing the same name are filed chronologically by date of birth. Some cards contain no birth or christening date, but in this space is written a marriage, death date, or other dated event, e.g., md. 5 Sept 1744, and this marriage date is filed chronologically as if it were a birth or christening date:

Byron, Elizabeth   chr. 9 Jan 1743
Brin, Elizabeth   md. 5 Sept 1744
Bryan, Elizabeth   b. 1746
Brian, Elizabeth   b. abt. 1748
Bryan, Elizabeth   b. 11 Jan 1748
O'Brian, Elizabeth chr. 6 Mar 1748

An approximated birth date on a T.I.B. card may not be the same as the known or approximated date used by the individual making the search. Therefore, a period of several years should be searched to allow for a difference in birth dates.

The filing system in the T.I.B. is basically one of combining surnames with like sounds regardless of spelling, e.g., the spelling of the surname Johnson is used in its proper alphabetical order and other spelling variations are filed with Johnson as though they were spelled the same. There are six blue cards in front of these "Johnson cards" which list all combinations of spellings used in the Johnson section. A white cross reference card is filed where the other spellings would normally occur in a strict alphabetical arrangement. Double consonants are filed as if they were single letters.

Much ordinance work was performed in the early days of the L.D.S. Church when the correct name was not known. The individual's proxy work was sometimes performed under the name of

Great-grandfather Hancock, Uncle Ivey, etc. Often just the surname is given preceded by Miss, Mr., or Mrs. These cards are filed at the beginning of each surname section.

Combinations of given names are filed together, and it is difficult to state the rules for all of these. The *Catalogue of Combined Given Names*, a compilation prepared by the employees of the T.I.B. for their use, is an aid in determining the standard combinations, e.g., Eliza and Elizabeth are considered two different names. Names combined under Eliza are as follows:

ELIZA	Eliese	Elize	Lise
	Elisa	Eliza	Liza
	Elisah	Elyza	Lize
	Elise	Lisa	Lysa
	Elizah	Lissa	Lyse

When searching in the T.I.B., all possible spellings and combinations should be considered. The T.I.B. card for E. Leroy Jensen was found under the name, Eleroy Jensen. Women were sometimes endowed under their married names, resulting in duplication of the endowment. The T.I.B. card of Mary Elizabeth Hunt, who married John Pulley, could be found under any of the following combinations:

Mary Elizabeth Hunt	Mary Elizabeth Pulley
Elizabeth Mary Hunt	Elizabeth Mary Pulley
Mary E. Hunt	Mary E. Pulley
Elizabeth M. Hunt	Elizabeth M. Pulley
M. E. Hunt	M. E. Pulley
E. M. Hunt	E. M. Pulley
Mary Hunt	Mary Pulley
Elizabeth Hunt	Elizabeth Pulley
Miss Hunt	Mrs. Pulley
	Mrs. John Pulley

It is also possible that the surnames Hunt and Pulley could be used together, e.g., Mary Hunt Pulley.

Sometimes a woman's T.I.B. card can be located by searching for the name of the wife as shown on the husband's T.I.B. card, e.g., the birth and marriage certificates established the fact that Helen Dunn was the wife of James Malcolm. A T.I.B. card was not found for Helen Dunn, but on James Malcolm's card, his wife's name was recorded as Ellen Malcolm, and her T.I.B. card was found under this name. This is an example of an error in spelling because of the silent "H" and a woman being endowed under her married name rather than maiden name.

AVAILABILITY

1. One can obtain xerox copies of T.I.B. cards by presenting to T.I.B. employees a family group record with the names for which information is desired underlined in red, or by completing an individual request form for each name. This service is available by correspondence. (See sample letter, Chapter 20.)

2. One can obtain information from the T.I.B. by engaging the services of an accredited researcher. (See sample letter, Chapter 20.)

GENEALOGICAL APPLICATION

1. Endowment dates are given. The T.I.B. cards showing endowment dates prior to 1927 were copied from the original temple records. Since 1927 the process has varied, and endowment dates have been recorded on the majority of the cards at the time of the endowment. The information recorded on the endowment card is the same as that in the original temple record. For this reason it is not necessary to check the original temple *endowment* record unless one suspects an error.

2. Baptism dates may be given. Many baptism dates for both the living and the dead were given from memory. No original temple baptism records were used in compiling the T.I.B. cards; however, some baptism dates were added to the cards at or near the time of baptism. For this reason original baptism records (either temple or ward records) should be consulted to verify baptism dates.

3. Sealing dates may be given. Sealing dates are not usually recorded on T.I.B. cards. Some T.I.B. cards contain only sealing information and have been indexed from early sealing records. (See Chapter 19.)

4. Clues are given concerning proxy baptisms. The name of the temple, dates of proxy baptisms (baptisms performed after the death of an individual), and the name of the heir or family representative aid in finding the original proxy baptism record for the individual as well as for relatives. When a proxy baptism date is indicated on a T.I.B. card, one should always search the original proxy baptism record of the respective temple for names of other relatives who were baptized on that same date. (See Chapter 19.)

5. Clues are given concerning proxy sealings. Proxy endowments and proxy sealings were frequently performed on or near the same day and in the same temple. Sealing records should be searched in the temple where the endowment was performed on or near the given endowment date. A sealing date many years after the endowment date(s) could indicate a repeat sealing and therefore, an invalid sealing date. (See Chapter 19.)

6. Cross reference is made to family group records in the Main Records Section (white and pink labeled binders) of the Church Records Archives. A "P" and/or "C" in the upper left-hand corner of a T.I.B. card indicates that the individual appears as a parent and/or child on a family group record(s) in the Main Records Section of the Church Records Archives. (See Chapter 13.)

7. The T.I.B. is an aid in establishing the spelling of names used on family group records in the Main Records Section of the Church Records Archives.

8. There may be information on T.I.B. cards which has not been repeated on the family group records in the Church Records Archives (all sections). The T.I.B. also includes information on individuals whose endowment work was performed prior to the establishment (1942) of the Main Records Section of the Church Records Archives.

9. The information given may be from a primary source. The T.I.B. cards often contain information an individual gave about himself or close relatives: brothers, sisters, aunts, uncles, cousins, parents, and grandparents.

10. General information is given on names, places, dates, and relationships which may verify, or add to, presently known information and provides clues to records to be searched in both the survey phase and the research phase.

11. The T.I.B. cards aid in preventing duplication of research and temple ordinance work on both L.D.S. and non-L.D.S. pedigrees.

12. The T.I.B. is used continuously in both the survey phase and the research phase. As family group records are completed and pedigrees extended, each new name should be checked in the T.I.B.

13. Reference is sometimes given to card-indexed pedigree charts. (See Chapter 13.)

GENEALOGICAL LIMITATIONS

1. The public does not have direct access to the T.I.B.

2. The information given is frequently inaccurate and incomplete.

3. The informant or source of the information is often unidentified.

4. Original baptism records are not indexed in the T.I.B. The date of baptism recorded on the T.I.B. card may have been given at the time of the endowment or at the time a family group record was submitted for processing rather than from the original baptism record.

5. Very few original sealing records are indexed, and there is uncertainty as to which sealing records are indexed.

6. Some T.I.B. cards are missing; others are misfiled. Often family records will indicate an endowment has been performed but

no card can be located. If a date is indicated, one should search the original endowment records for the specific temple. (See Chapter 19.)

PROJECT ASSIGNMENT

1. Obtain copies of T.I.B. cards for individuals on the family group record selected for research in Chapter 6.

Chapter Thirteen

CHURCH RECORDS ARCHIVES

■ The Church Records Archives is the term used to refer to the pedigree charts and family group records filed in the library of The Genealogical Society. Pedigree charts have been submitted for the purpose of filing only, while family group records have been submitted either for filing only or for processing for temple ordinance work and then filing. Many of these records which were formerly available in binders are now available on microfilm.

PEDIGREE CHARTS

Between 1924 and 1962 pedigree charts were accepted by the library of The Genealogical Society for filing:

Card-indexed: These pedigree charts were the earliest ones received by The Genealogical Society, were filed in binders, and recently microfilmed. The binders were assigned a letter of the alphabet with a "7" prefix ranging from "7" to "7R," and each pedigree chart was then assigned a page number. An index card was made for each person on each pedigree chart giving the number of the binder, page number of the pedigree chart, and number of the individual; e.g., 7E-460-1 indicates that in binder 7E, on chart (page) number 460, the individual indexed is number 1. The entire number must be copied from the index card to be used as a reference in locating the correct microfilm. Numbers not prefixed by "7" refer to an out-dated filing system and need not be copied.

Alphabetized: When it became impossible to make an index card for each individual on each pedigree chart, the charts were filed alphabetically by individual #1 on the pedigree. These have been microfilmed in two divisions; the first includes pedigree charts which were once filed in binders; the second, pedigree charts which were not in binders.

Miscellaneous: There are some pedigree charts on file which were submitted by private researchers and family organizations and are usually organized alphabetically by individual #1 on the pedigree chart. These pedigree charts are available on microfilm.

FAMILY GROUP RECORDS

Family group records are submitted to The Genealogical Society either for filing only or for processing for temple ordinances and then filing. Some family group records are presented at the temple for temple ordinances and then sent to The Genealogical Society for filing. Those family group records for filing only are in the Patrons Section and include family group records for names of individuals not eligible for temple work at the time of filing. Those family group records which have been submitted for temple ordinances and filed are in a processed section.

Family group records at The Genealogical Society are filed in alphabetical order by the surname of the husband. When two or more husbands have the same name, the family group records are filed chronologically (earliest birth date first). When no husband is listed, the record is filed by the name of the wife. The T.I.B., where cards are filed phonetically rather than alphabetically, is a valuable tool in determining the spelling used in the Main Records Section (finished and unfinished section) of the Church Records Archives.

Family group records are located at the library of The Genealogical Society according to the dates they were submitted and the condition of the ordinance work.

Patrons Section: 1924-1962: Family group records have been accepted in the Church Records Archives for filing since 1924. In 1928 the Patrons Section was established and those family group records received prior to this time were placed in the Patrons Section. These and subsequent records received through 1950 were filed in binders and microfilmed. The family group records received from 1950 to 1962 recently have been integrated into this section and the section re-microfilmed.

Since 1962—: Family group records submitted for filing after 1962 are located in binders (yellow labels) in the archive reading room. This includes the three- and four-generation family group records submitted under the direction of the Priesthood. The three- and four-generation family group records have also been microfilmed.

Miscellaneous: There are some family group records on file in binders (yellow, white labels) and on microfilm which were submitted by private researchers and family organizations.

Processed Section: Finished, 1942-   : Family group records submitted for processing after 1942 for which all ordinance dates have been completed are filed in binders (pink labels). Prior to 1942 family group records submitted for processing were returned to the patron or compiler and no copy was retained by The Genealogical Society.

Unfinished, 1942-   : Family group records submitted for processing after 1942 and for which some ordinance dates have not been completed are filed in binders (white labels).

When all ordinance dates are completed on a family group record in the unfinished section, it is transferred to the finished section. The finished and unfinished binders are referred to as the Main Records Section of the Church Records Archives. Cross reference is made on the T.I.B. cards to these two sections by the use of the "P" and "C."

A special feature of the Main Records Section is the cross reference from one family group record to another. An asterisk (*) after the name of an individual indicates that he appears on another family group record in either the finished or unfinished sections.

Sealing, 1956-   : Family group records in this section were compiled from family records which gave a baptism and endowment date but no sealing date, and therefore, were submitted for sealings only. Also included in this section are family group records for previously married couples who later went to the temple for sealings and presented their family group record at the temple rather than at The Genealogical Society. These family group records are filed in binders (orange labels).

AVAILABILITY

Archive Section	Binders at library, The Geneal. Soc.	Microfilm
Card-indexed Pedigree Charts		X
Alphabetized Pedigree Charts		X (two divisions)
Miscellaneous Pedigree Charts		X
Patrons Family Group Records (1924-1962)		X (two divisions)
Patron's Family Group Records (1962-)	X (yellow labels)	three- and four- generation, only
Patrons Miscellaneous Family Group Records	X (yellow, white labels)	X
Finished Family Group Records (1942-)	X (pink labels)	
Unfinished Family Group Records (1942-)	X (white labels)	
Sealing Family Group Records (1956-)	X (orange labels)	

Xerox copies of family group records which are in binders at the library of The Genealogical Society may be obtained by corresponding with the Public Service Department. (See sample letter, Chapter 20.) The patron must state the name of the husband and wife and the birth date of the husband. Reference should be made to spellings of names and any "P" and "C" notations as found in the T.I.B.

GENEALOGICAL APPLICATION

1. General information is given on names, places, dates, and relationships which may verify, or add to, presently known information and provides clues to further research.

2. The address of the patron or compiler is valuable for contacting other individuals doing research on the same pedigree problem. The patron or compiler may have hired research through the Research Department of The Genealogical Society where there may be a file. (See Chapter 11.)

3. Direct reference may be given to files in the Research Department of The Genealogical Society. This is indicated near the address of the patron by the initials (LMT) of the employee of the Research Department. (See Chapter 11.)

4. Family group records are valuable for listing names of children not presently known to the researcher. There may be T.I.B. cards for some of these children; however, those who died under the age of eight would not have a card in the T.I.B.

5. Family group records may contain baptism and sealing dates not recorded in the T.I.B. This is particularly true of the patrons section.

6. The name of the heir or family representative is given which is necessary for using indexes to temple ordinance records. (See Chapter 19.)

7. Through use of asterisks (*) in the Main Records Section (finished and unfinished sections) one can frequently trace a pedigree for several generations.

GENEALOGICAL LIMITATIONS

1. Information is often inaccurate and incomplete.

2. Frequently ordinances are repeated, and the recorded ordinance dates may not be valid.

3. Some family group records are misfiled or missing.

4. The alphabetical arrangement could be a limitation if one is not aware of the spelling of the name as recorded in the Church Records Archives.

PROJECT ASSIGNMENTS

1. Check the pedigree sections of the Church Records Archives for the surnames indicated on the family group record selected for research in Chapter 6.

2. Obtain copies of family group records containing information pertinent to the individuals whose names appear on the family group record selected for research.

Chapter Fourteen

CARD INDEXES TO MISCELLANEOUS RECORDS

■ Several card indexes have been prepared by employees of the Church Historian's Office and The Genealogical Society and these indexes are considered L.D.S. Church record sources. Each index refers to more than one record source, and to both L.D.S. and non-L.D.S. Church records, and records of both the survey phase and the research phase.

ADVANTAGES OF AN INDEX

1. The alphabetical arrangement saves time because it is not necessary to search an entire record page by page.

2. An index makes reference to the original source which should always be searched as it may contain additional information.

LIMITATIONS OF AN INDEX

1. There may be copying errors and omissions.

2. Names are listed alphabetically according to spelling in the record sources, and often no allowance is made for spelling variations and cross references.

3. Errors and omissions may occur in alphabetizing.

4. Females may be referred to by maiden and/or married surname(s).

SURNAME CARD INDEX

Origin and Contents: The Surname Card Index (sometimes referred to as the Index File or Surname File) is an index of names of persons compiled from parts of books or records, e.g., periodical articles, Bible records, and biographical sketches. Names included in the index are from sources in the library of The Genealogical Society. Information on the index card varies and may include the following:

1. Surname or complete name.
2. Date of birth.
3. Place of birth.
4. Date of death.
5. Place of death.
6. Date of marriage.
7. Place of marriage.
8. Name of spouse.
9. Type of record indexed.
10. Name of record indexed.
11. Call number, library of The Genealogical Society.

Availability:

1. Original index—library of The Genealogical Society.

Genealogical Application:

1. The surname card index refers to the original record where more biographical information may be found. Often this information is not easily located through the dictionary card catalogue.

Genealogical Limitations:

1. Index cards have not been made for each book or record in the library of The Genealogical Society.

2. There is uncertainty as to which records are indexed.

EARLY CHURCH INFORMATION CARD INDEX

Origin and Contents: The Early Church Information Card Index (sometimes referred to as the Early Church Information File) is an index of names of persons compiled from various L.D.S. Church and early Utah records. The index cards list the following references:

1. Deaths of Mormon pioneers in 1846, 1847, and 1848 as inscribed on the Mount Pisgah Monument.

2. Inscriptions from tombstones in the old Nauvoo, Illinois Cemetery.

3. Early High Priests and Seventies Quorum records.

4. Springville City, Utah County, Utah records beginning March 20, 1851.

5. Payson City, Utah County, Utah records beginning early.

6. Spanish Fork City, Utah County, Utah records beginning early.

7. Patriarchal Blessings (uncertainty as to exact volumes).

8. Union, Pottawattamie County, Iowa, branch records 1853-1855.

9. L.D.S. Church Ward records: 16th and 17th Wards, Salt Lake City; Mapleton Ward, Utah Stake; Richfield 1st, 2nd, and 3rd Wards, Sevier Stake; Malad 1st Ward, Malad Stake; Granger Ward, Granite Stake; Redmese Ward, Young Stake; Cowley Ward, Big Horn Stake; Hunter Ward, Granite Stake; Ephraim North Ward, South Sanpete Stake; Springville Ward, Kolob Stake; 4th Ward, Utah Stake; Hyde Park Ward, Cache Stake; West Weber Ward, Weber Stake; Lynne Ward, Weber Stake; Glenwood Ward, Sevier

Stake; Granger Ward, Cottonwood Stake; Pleasant Green Ward, Salt Lake Stake; Lewisville Ward, Rigby Stake; Daniels Ward, Malad Stake; and references to Nebo Stake, no ward given.

10. Extracts of births, marriages, and deaths from early L.D.S. Church newspapers: "Evening and Morning Star" (Independence, Missouri), 1832-1833 and (Kirtland, Ohio), 1833-1834; "L.D.S. Messenger and Advocate" (Kirtland, Ohio), 1834-1836; "The Elder's Journal" (Kirtland, Ohio), 1837-1838 and (Far West), 1838; "Times and Seasons" (Commerce or Nauvoo, Illinois), 1839-1846; "The Wasp" (Nauvoo, Illinois), 1843; "Nauvoo Neighbor" (Nauvoo, Illinois), 1843-1845; "Frontier Guardian" (Kanesville or Council Bluffs, Iowa), 1849-1852.

Information on the cards varies and may include the following:

1. Name of individual.
2. Father's name.
3. Mother's name.
4. Date of birth.
5. Place of birth.
6. Date of L.D.S. baptism.
7. By whom baptized.
8. Place of baptism.
9. Date of confirmation.
10. By whom confirmed.
11. Place of marriage.
12. Date of marriage.
13. Name of spouse.
14. Date of death.
15. Place of death.
16. Date of burial.
17. Place of burial.
18. Date of endowment.
19. Date sealed to spouse.
20. Date sealed to parents.
21. References: name of record, page number.

Availability:
1. Original index—library of The Genealogical Society

Genealogical Application:
1. The Early Church Information Card Index refers to the original record source where additional information may be recorded.

2. The informant was often closely associated with the event.

3. General information is given on names, places, dates, and relationships which may verify, or add to, presently known information and provides clues to further research.

Genealogical Limitations:
1. Only a small portion of L.D.S. Church and early Utah records have been indexed.

2. There is uncertainty as to which records are indexed.

MARRIAGE LICENSE CARD INDEX

Origin and Contents: The Marriage License Card Index (sometimes referred to as the Miscellaneous Marriage Index) is an index of names of persons compiled from marriage license records in some county courthouses in Utah, Idaho, and Wyoming. (At one time this index was combined with the Early Church Information Card Index resulting in a total of 150,000 cards). References on the cards indicate the early marriage license records of the following counties have been indexed: Millard, Salt Lake, Utah, Sevier, Summit, Weber, Box Elder, Morgan, and Sanpete, Utah; Lincoln, Wyoming; and Lemhi, and Franklin, Idaho.

The card index is arranged alphabetically by the surname of the individual. Information on the cards varies and may include the following:

1. Name in full.
2. Date of birth.
3. Place of birth.
4. Residence and occupation.

5. Father's name.
6. Place of father's birth.
7. Mother's maiden name.
8. Place of mother's birth.
9. Date of license.
10. Where license issued.
11. Date of marriage.
12. Place of marriage.
13. By whom married.
14. Name of spouse.
15. Single, widowed, or divorced.
16. Number of marriage (1st, 2nd, etc.)
17. Name of county.
18. Reference: book number and page number.

Availability:
1. Original index—library of The Genealogical Society.

Genealogical Application:
1. The Marriage License Card Index refers to the original marriage license records.

2. Information may be from a primary source as the informant was often closely associated with the event.

3. General information is given on names, places, dates, and relationships which may verify, or add to, presently known information and provides clues to further research.

Genealogical Limitations:
1. Only a small portion of Utah, Idaho, and Wyoming marriage license records are indexed.

2. There is uncertainty as to which counties are included in the index.

3. There is uncertainty as to the time period included.

OBITUARY CARD INDEX

Origin and Contents: The Obituary Card Index (sometimes referred to as Obituary File or Obituary Index) is an index of names of persons whose obituaries have appeared in Salt Lake City newspapers and other miscellaneous records: "Deseret News" (weekly, 1850-1888); "The Deseret Evening News" (1867-1920); "Deseret News" (1920-1952); "Deseret News-Salt Lake Telegram" (1952-1961; "Deseret News" (1961-   ) "The Deseret News Weekly" (1888-1898); "The Salt Lake Tribune" (1877-   ); *The Journal History of The Church of Jesus Christ of Latter-day Saints;* "Times and Seasons," *The Improvement Era;* "Elder's Journal," Provo 2nd Ward records, etc.

Information on the index cards varies and may include the following:

1. Name of the deceased.
2. Age of deceased.
3. Date of death.
4. Place of death.
5. Date of obituary.
6. Name of newspaper.
7. Name of father.
8. Name of mother.
9. Date of birth.
10. Place of birth.
11. Cause of death.
12. References: page number and column number. (Obituaries in early newspapers often are located on different pages).

Availability:

1. Microfilmed copy of index to 1963—library of The Genealogical Society.

2. Original index to present—Church Historian's Office.

Genealogical Application:

1. The Obituary Card Index refers to the original record where the obituary with additional information may be found.

2. Obituaries may appear for individuals who resided in other areas; these are often brief notices which lead to a more detailed obituary in the home town newspaper.

Genealogical Limitations:

1. The sources indicated on the index cards are not completely indexed.

2. There is uncertainty as to which sources are indexed.

PROJECT ASSIGNMENT

1. Continue research on the family group record selected in Chapter 6 by searching the following card indexes:

    a. Surname Card Index.

    b. Early Church Information Card Index.

    c. Marriage License Card Index.

    d. Obituary Card Index.

Chapter Fifteen

L.D.S. CHURCH EMIGRATION, IMMIGRATION, AND MIGRATION

■ On April 6, 1830, in Fayette Township, Seneca County, New York, The Church of Jesus Christ of Latter-day Saints was organized under the direction of Joseph Smith. Membership grew rapidly, and in December, 1830, the first direct commandment was given that the members of the L.D.S. Church should gather together; the New York saints (members) were instructed to move to Ohio. During the winter of 1830-1831, the majority migrated to Kirtland, Geauga (now Lake) County, Ohio. Joseph Smith arrived there with his family about February 1, 1831.

For a time it appeared that the members of the L.D.S. Church would long enjoy their community at Kirtland, but their stay was short. In 1837, Joseph Smith and many of his followers, because of persecutions, fled to Far West, Caldwell County, Missouri, and joined with a group of saints, some of whom had been in Missouri since 1831 and who had migrated from Colesville, Broome County, New York about the same time Joseph Smith had moved to Kirtland. As a small group, they had first settled about twelve miles from Independence, Jackson County, Missouri. By 1833 they had grown to a body of about 1200, and at that time were driven from their homes and settled temporarily in Clay County, just north of Jackson County, Missouri. From there, in 1836, they moved to Caldwell County and founded the city of Far West.

There were constant persecutions in these early days, and Joseph Smith's presence at Far West seemed only to further agitate the anti-Mormons. In the autumn of 1838, the entire church membership was expelled from the State of Missouri by order of Governor Lilburn W. Boggs.

While the saints were being forced to leave Missouri, Joseph Smith and several other L.D.S. Church leaders were betrayed and taken to Liberty Jail in Clay County, Missouri, where they were held on false charges of murder, arson, and treason. Several months later they escaped and joined the main body of The Church in Quincy, Adams County, Illinois, and vicinity. Soon afterwards, the members moved to Commerce, Hancock County, Illinois and built the city of Nauvoo.

On June 27, 1844, Joseph Smith was martyred at Carthage Jail, near Nauvoo, Hancock County, Illinois, while awaiting trial on false charges of treason against the State of Illinois. After the death of Joseph Smith, persecutions continued until the saints were compelled to leave Nauvoo.

On February 4, 1846, the first of 20,000 saints started the gradual migration from Nauvoo by crossing the Mississippi River from Illinois to Iowa. Some 400 to 500 families left Nauvoo during the first two weeks in February and gathered at a point about 9 miles from the Mississippi River on a stream called Sugar Creek. After the arrival of Brigham Young on February 15, they organized into groups, and on March 1, packed their tents and other belongings and started westward.

The first 50 saints arrived at Garden Grove, Decatur County, Iowa, about 144 miles from Nauvoo on April 24, 1846. This was the first place to be established as a temporary settlement. At Mt. Pisgah, Union County, about 30 miles west of Garden Grove, the second settlement was established and several thousand acres of land were fenced for cultivation. Mt. Pisgah became a place to replenish diminished supplies for thousands of saints who later migrated across the plains. (This settlement was broken up in 1852 when Brigham Young called the remaining people at Mt. Pisgah to Utah.)

It has been estimated that by May 18, 1846, there were about 5,000 saints in various locations on the plains of Iowa. The first pioneer company reached Council Bluffs, Pottawattamie County, Iowa on June 14, 1846. They named the settlement Miller's Hollow, later it was named Kanesville, and after the L.D.S. pioneers left, it was given its present name of Council Bluffs.

On June 29, 1846, a ferry boat was launched and on July 2, Brigham Young with his family, wagons, teams, and traveling equipment crossed the Missouri River from Iowa to Nebraska. A number of other saints followed. They traveled four miles inland and formed a camp at Cold Springs. In September, 1846, more saints began to locate at Winter Quarters, Omaha County, at what is now Florence, Douglas County, Nebraska. There were 15,000 saints gathered in the Council Bluffs-Winter Quarters area in the fall of 1846.

The following excerpt is quoted from a letter signed by Brigham Young and Willard Richards:

"Our present design is to settle our families at this point in such a manner that we can leave them one season, or more if necessity requires, and fit out a company of able men with our best teams and seeds, and at the earliest moment in the ensuing spring, start for the Bear River Valley, find a location, plant seeds, build homes, etc., and the next season be ready to receive our families into comfortable habitation, filled with plenty of bread, etc.

"We design to build log cabins here and make every possible exertion this winter for an abundant harvest here next summer. Should all these calculations succeed you will perceive that we shall need to carry little bread stuff across the mountains."[1]

---

[1]Preston Nibley, *Exodus to Greatness* (Salt Lake City: Deseret News Press, 1947), p. 236.

On April 14, 1847, the first company of 148 persons left Winter Quarters, traveled along the northern side of the Platte River to Fort Laramie (Wyoming). On July 24, 1847, the first L.D.S. pioneers entered the Great Salt Lake Valley in what is now the State of Utah. Many companies of saints were to follow, and by 1849 there were about 8,000 people in Utah, more than 8,000 on the plains enroute to Utah, and 30,000 L.D.S. Church members in Great Britain. By 1869 the population of what is now the State of Utah was 80,000, and 6,000 had died enroute.

Some British converts had immigrated to the United States as early as 1840; the first L.D.S. organized group left Liverpool in June of that year. By June 1841 more than 1,000 persons had emigrated from England, but not all had been accounted for or named in L.D.S. Church emigration records as some sailed independently rather than with L.D.S. Church organized companies to New York, Philadelphia, Boston and other American ports. On December 23, 1847, a general epistle from the Council of the Twelve Apostles at Winter Quarters instructed the saints in England, Scotland, Ireland, Wales, and adjacent islands and countries to immigrate as speedily as possible to the vicinity of Winter Quarters. In order to save expense, they were instructed to go by ship to New Orleans, and from there directly to Council Bluffs, Iowa.[2]

The first company of emigrants from continental Europe was from the Scandinavian Mission, and sailed on the "Italy," on March 11, 1852. The second was from Scandinavia also, then the third included seventeen persons from the German Mission who sailed from Liverpool in August or September of 1853. Records of these persons were kept by the L.D.S. agent at the Liverpool office, and the majority of these emigrants after leaving their homeland, re-embarked at Liverpool.

L.D.S. Church sponsored emigrants from European countries were organized under the direction of a superintendent or agent who received applications from converts and chartered sailing vessels. Often the majority of passengers on a ship were from the same

---

[2]Edward W. Tullidge, *History of Salt Lake City* (Salt Lake City: Star Printing Company, 1886), p. 98.

conference or district. The passengers on a ship were called a company, and were under the supervision of a president and counselors. The companies were further divided into groups, each group being under the supervision of a president. A similar organization was used crossing the plains; i.e., families of hundreds, fifties, and tens.

The first immigrants who disembarked on the east coast of the United States traveled overland to meet the main body of the saints. After the headquarters of The Church were established in Nauvoo, most of the L.D.S. sponsored immigrants arrived at New Orleans, Louisiana, and then proceeded up the Mississippi River to Nauvoo. In 1853 the emigrants from Europe journeyed up the Mississippi River to Keokuk, Iowa, where the trek across the plains began. In 1854 the outfitting place for crossing the plains was Westport (now within the limits of Kansas City, Missouri), and in 1855, Mormon Grove, a few miles west of Atchison, Kansas. When it was discovered that the people from northern Europe could not endure the climate of the southern states, as cholera and yellow fever caused numerous fatalities, the emigrants, instead of landing at New Orleans, were landed at New York, Philadelphia, and Boston. From these seaport towns the journey was continued by rail to Iowa City or places where the railroad could be utilized.[3]

The journey by rail ended at an L.D.S. Church outfitting station where the emigrants obtained supplies and covered wagons to continue on their journey to Great Salt Lake Valley. To help those persons with little means, the first of ten handcart companies was organized in 1856, the last one in 1860.

Pioneers continued to arrive in Great Salt Lake Valley with covered wagons until 1868, but the length of the wagon journey was gradually shortened as the Union Pacific Railroad extended westward. By 1864 the L.D.S. Church outfitting station was in Wyoming, Nebraska, and by 1868, in Laramie City, Wyoming. The last L.D.S. Church organized company to travel overland by covered wagon left Benton, Wyoming on September 1, 1868, and arrived in Great Salt Lake Valley on September 24. In October 1868, trains ran to Bridger's Pass. The first train came into Ogden, March 8,

---

[3]Kate B. Carter, *Heart Throbs of the West* (Salt Lake City: Daughters of Utah Pioneers, 1943), vol. 4, pp. 145-146.

1869. Many trains made the trip into Utah before the "Golden Spike" ceremony at Promontory on May 10, 1869.

Other pioneers important in L.D.S. Church history include the Samuel Brannan group of 235 L.D.S. Church members who sailed on board the "Brooklyn" from New York on February 4, 1846, around the Cape in South America and up the coast to the San Francisco area of California, and the nearly 600 persons, including some women and children, in the Mormon Battalion who left Council Bluffs, Iowa, July 18, 1846.

L.D.S. CHURCH IMMIGRATION TO UTAH[4]
Organized Companies Overland

Outfitting Station	Date of Departure	Captain of Company	Persons	Wagons	Arrival in Great Salt Lake Valley
Winter Quarters, Neb.	1847 April 14	Brigham Young	148	72	July 24
Winter Quarters, Neb.	1847 June 17	Daniel Spencer Capt. 1st Hundred			
		Peregrine Sessions Capt. 1st Fifty	185	75	Sept. 24
		Ira Eldredge Capt. 2nd Fifty	177	76	Sept. 19
Winter Quarters, Neb.	1847 June 17	Edward Hunter Capt. 2nd Hundred			
		Joseph Horne Capt. 1st Fifty	197	72	Sept. 29
		Jacob Foutz Capt. 2nd Fifty	155	67	Oct. 1
Winter Quarters, Neb.	1847 June 17	Jedediah M. Grant Capt. 3rd Hundred			
		Joseph B. Noble Capt. 1st Fifty	171		Oct. 2
		Willard Snow Capt. 2nd Fifty	160		Oct. 4
Winter Quarters, Neb.	1847 June 17	Abraham O. Smoot Capt. 4th Hundred			
		George B. Wallace Capt. 1st Fifty	223		Sept. 25
		Samuel Russell Capt. 2nd Fifty	95		Sept. 25
Winter Quarters, Neb.	1847 June 17	Charles C. Rich Capt. of the Guard	126		Oct. 2
Winter Quarters, Neb.	1848 May 26	Brigham Young Capt. 1st Division	1220		Sept. 21
Winter Quarters, Neb.	1848 May 29	Heber C. Kimball Capt. 2nd Division	662		Sept. 23
Winter Quarters, Neb.	1848 June 30	Willard Richards Capt. 3rd Division	526		Oct. 19
Kanesville, Iowa	1849 June 6	Orson Spencer		100	Sept. 22

[4]Ibid., pp. 338-342

L. D. S. CHURCH IMMIGRATION TO UTAH
Organized Companies Overland

Outfitting Station	Date of Departure	Captain of Company	Persons	Wagons	Arrival in Great Salt Lake Valley
Kanesville, Iowa	1849 July 12	Allen Taylor	500	100	Oct. 1
Kanesville, Iowa	1849 July 10	Silas Richards			Oct. 12
Kanesville, Iowa	1849 July 4	George A. Smith Ezra T. Benson	447	120	Oct. 27
Kanesville, Iowa	1849 April 19	Howard Egan Ind. Co.	57	22	Aug. 7
Kanesville, Iowa	1850 June 3	Milo Andrus	206	51	Aug. 30
Kanesville, Iowa	1850 June 7	Benjamin Hawkins		150	Sept. 9
Kanesville, Iowa	1850 June 12	Aaron Johnson			Sept. 12
Kanesville, Iowa	1850 June	James Pace		100	Sept. 20
Kanesville, Iowa	1850 July 4	Edward Hunter (P. E. Fund)	261	67	Oct. 13
Kanesville, Iowa	1850 June 15	Joseph Young		42	Oct. 1
Kanesville, Iowa	1850 June 15	Warren Foote		105	Sept. 17
Kanesville, Iowa	1850 June 20	Wilford Woodruff		44	Oct. 14
Kanesville, Iowa	1850 June 20	Stephen Markham		50	Oct. 1
Kanesville, Iowa	1850 June 15	David Evans		54	Sept. 15
Kanesville, Iowa	1851 May 1	John G. Smith		150	Sept. 23
Kanesville, Iowa	1851 June 21	James W. Cummings		100	Oct. 5
Kanesville, Iowa	1851 June 29	Easton Kelsey		100	Sept. 23
Kanesville, Iowa	1851 July 7	John Brown (P. E. Fund)		50	Sept. 28
Kanesville, Iowa	1851	George W. Oman			Sept. 1
Kanesville, Iowa	1851	Morris Phelps			Sept. 28
Kanesville, Iowa	1852 May 30	James W. Bay	190		Aug. 13
Kanesville, Iowa	1852 May 29	James J. Jepson			Sept. 10
Kanesville, Iowa	1852 June 7	Thomas D. Howell	200		Sept. 27
Kanesville, Iowa	1852 June 10	Joseph Outhouse	225	50	Sept. 6
Kanesville, Iowa	1852 June	John Tidwell	340	32	Sept. 15
Kanesville, Iowa	1852 June	David Wood	260		Oct. 1
Kanesville, Iowa	1852 June	Henry B. M. Jolley	340		Sept. 15
Kanesville, Iowa	1852 June	Isaac W. Stewart	245		Aug. 28
Kanesville, Iowa	1852 May 15	Benjamin Gardner	241	45	Sept. 24
Kanesville, Iowa	1852 June	James McGaw	239	54	Sept. 20
Kanesville, Iowa	1852 June	Harmon Cutler	262	63	Sept.
Kanesville, Iowa	1852 July 5	John B. Walker	250		Oct. 5
Kanesville, Iowa	1852 July	Robert Weimer	230		Sept. 15
Kanesville, Iowa	1852 June	Uriah Curtis	365		Oct. 1
Kanesville, Iowa	1852 June	Isaac Bullock	175		Sept. 21
Kanesville, Iowa	1852 June	James C. Snow	250		Oct. 9
Kanesville, Iowa	1852 July	Eli B. Kelsey	100		Oct. 16
Kanesville, Iowa	1852 June	Henry W. Miller	220		Sept. 21
Kanesville, Iowa	1852 July	Allen Weeks	110		October
Kanesville, Iowa	1852 June	Abraham O. Smoot (P. E. Fund)	250	31	Sept. 3
Kanesville, Iowa	1852 June 4	Thomas Marsden		10	Sept. 2
Six Mile Grove, Iowa	1853 June 1	David Wilkin	122	28	Sept. 9
Six Mile Grove, Iowa	1853 June 9	John A. Miller John W. Cooley	282	70	Sept. 9
Keokuk, Iowa	1853 May 18	Jesse W. Crosby	79	12	Sept. 10
Kanesville, Iowa	1853 June	Moses Clawson	295	56	Sept. 15
Keokuk, Iowa	1853 June 3	Jacob Gates	262	38	Sept. 26
Keokuk, Iowa	1853 May 21	John E. Forsgren	294	34	Sept. 30
Keokuk, Iowa	1853 July 1	Henry Ettleman	40	11	Oct. 1

L. D. S. CHURCH IMMIGRATION TO UTAH
Organized Companies Overland

Outfitting Station	Date of Departure	Captain of Company	Persons	Wagons	Arrival in Great Salt Lake Valley
Kanesville, Iowa	1853 July 13	Vincent Shurtliff			Sept. 30
Kanesville, Iowa	1853 July 11	Joseph W. Young	321	42	Oct. 10
Keokuk, Iowa	1853 June 3	Cyrus H. Wheelock	400	52	Oct. 16
Kanesville, Iowa	1853 June 3	Claudius V. Spencer (P. E. Fund)	250	40	Sept. 24
Kanesville, Iowa	1853 July 14	Appleton M. Harmon	200	22	Oct. 16
Keokuk, Iowa	1853 July 1	John Brown	228		Oct. 17
Kansas City, Mo. (Westport)	1854 June 15	Hans Peter Olsen	550	69	Oct. 5
Kansas City, Mo. (Westport)	1854 June 17	James Brown (P. E. Fund)	300	42	Oct. 3
Kansas City, Mo. (Westport)	1854 June 17	Darwin Richardson (P. E. Fund)	300	40	Sept. 30
Kansas City, Mo. (Westport)	1854 June 16	Job Smith	217	45	Sept. 23
Kansas City, Mo. (Westport)	1854 July 2	Daniel Garn (P. E. Fund)	447	40	Oct. 1
Kansas City, Mo. (Westport)	1854 July 14	Robert L. Campbell	400		Oct. 28
Kansas City, Mo. (Westport)	1854 July	Ezra T. Benson	(mostly freight)		Oct. 3
Kansas City, Mo. (Westport)	1854 July	Wm. Empey		45	Oct. 24
Mormon Grove, Kas.	1855 June 7	John Hindley	206	46	Sept. 3
Mormon Grove, Kas.	1855 June 13	Jacob F. Secrist	368	51	Sept. 1
Mormon Grove, Kas.	1855 June 15	Seth M. Blair	89	38	Sept. 11
Mormon Grove, Kas.	1855 July 1	Richard Ballantyne (P. E. Fund)	402	45	Sept. 25
Mormon Grove, Kas.	1855 July 4	Moses F. Thurston	134	29	Sept. 28
Mormon Grove, Kas.	1855 July 28	C. A. Harper	305	39	Oct. 29
Mormon Grove, Kas.	1855 July 31	Isaac Allred	61	34	Nov. 2
Mormon Grove, Kas.	1855 Aug. 5	Milo Andrus (P. E. Fund)	452	48	Oct. 24
Iowa City, Iowa	1856 June 9	Edmund Ellsworth	275	4 52*	Sept. 26
Iowa City, Iowa	1856 June 11	Daniel McArthur	222	4 48*	Sept. 26
Iowa City, Iowa	1856 June 23	Edward Bunker	300	5 60*	Oct. 2
Iowa City, Iowa	1856 July 15	James G. Willie	500	5 120*	Nov. 9
Iowa City, Iowa	1856 Aug. 25	Edward Martin	575	7 146*	Nov. 30
Florence, Neb.	1856 June 5	Philemon C. Merrill	200	50	Aug. 13-18
Florence, Neb.	1856 June 10	Knud Peterson	320	60	Sept. 20
Florence, Neb.	1856 June 15	John Banks	300	60	Oct. 1
Iowa City, Iowa	1856 July 30	Wm. B. Hodgetts	150	33	Dec. 10-15
Iowa City, Iowa	1856 Aug. 1	John A. Hunt	300	56	Dec. 10-15
Iowa City, Iowa	1857 May 22	Israel Evans	149	1 28*	Sept. 11
Iowa City, Iowa	1857 June 15	Christian Christiansen	330	3 68*	Sept. 13

*Number of handcarts

L. D. S. CHURCH IMMIGRATION TO UTAH
Organized Companies Overland

Outfitting Station	Date of Departure	Captain of Company	Persons	Wagons	Arrival in Great Salt Lake Valley
Florence, Neb.	1857 June 13	Wm. Walker	86	28	Sept. 4
Iowa City, Iowa	1857 June	Jesse B. Martin	192	34	Sept. 12
Iowa City, Iowa	1857 June 15	Matthias Cowley	198	31	Sept. 13
Iowa City, Iowa	1857 June	Jacob Hoffheins	204	41	Sept. 21
Texas	1857 July	Homer Duncan			Sept. 14, 20
Iowa City, Iowa	1857 June	Wm. G. Young	55	19	Sept. 26
Iowa City, Iowa	1858 June 8	Horace S. Eldredge	39	13	July 9
Iowa City, Iowa	1858 June 9	Russell K. Homer	60		Oct. 6
Florence, Neb.	1858 July	Iver N. Iversen	50	8	Sept. 20
Florence, Neb.	1859 June 9	George Rowley	255	8 60*	Sept. 4
Florence, Neb.	1859 June 13	James Brown, III	387	66	Aug. 29
Florence, Neb.	1859 June	Horton D. Haight	154	71	Sept. 1
Florence, Neb.	1859 June 28	Robert F. Neslen	380	56	Sept. 15
Florence, Neb.	1859 June 26	Edward Stevenson	285	54	Sept. 16
Florence, Neb.	1860 June 6	Daniel Robinson	235	6 43*	Aug. 27
Florence, Neb.	1860 July 6	Oscar O. Stoddard	126	6 22*	Sept. 24
Florence, Neb.	1860 May 30	Warren Walling	160	30	Aug. 9
Florence, Neb.	1860 June 17	James D. Ross	249	36	Sept. 3
Florence, Neb.	1860 June 19	Jesse Murphy	279	40	Aug. 30
Florence, Neb.	1860 June 15	John Smith	359	39	Sept. 1
Florence, Neb.	1860 July 20	William Budge	400	55	Oct. 5
Florence, Neb.	1860 July 3	John Taylor	123		Sept. 17
Florence, Neb.	1860 July 23	Joseph W. Young	100	50	Oct. 3
Florence, Neb.	1860 June	Franklin Brown	60	abt. 10	Aug. 27
Florence, Neb.	1861 May 29	David H. Cannon	225	57	Aug. 16
Florence, Neb.	1861 June 7	Job Pingree	abt. 150	36	Aug. 2
Florence, Neb.	1861 June 20	Peter Ranck	abt. 100	20	Sept. 8
Florence, Neb.		Homer Duncan	258	47	Sept. 13
Florence, Neb.	1861 June 30	Ira Eldredge	abt. 300	70	Aug. 22
Florence, Neb.	1861 July	Milo Andrus	620	38	Sept. 12
Florence, Neb.	1861 July	Thomas Woolley	abt. 150	30	Sept.
Florence, Neb.	1861 July 9	Joseph Horne	abt. 350	62	Sept. 13
Florence, Neb.	1861 July 13	Samuel A. Woolley	338	70	Sept. 22
		Joseph Porter	Included in S. Woolley Co.		
Florence, Neb.	1861 July	John R. Murdock	abt. 500	33	Sept. 12
Florence, Neb.	1861 July 11	Joseph W. Young	abt. 300	90	Sept. 23
		Ancel P. Harmon	Included in Jos. W. Young Co.		
		Heber P. Kimball	Included in Jos. W. Young Co.		
Florence, Neb.	1861 July 16	Sixtus E. Johnson	200	52	Sept. 27
Florence, Neb.	1862 June 17	Lewis Brunson	212	48	Aug. 29
Florence, Neb.	1862 July	James Wareham	250	46	Sept. 26
Florence, Neb.	1862 July 14	Christian A. Madsen	264	40	Sept. 23
Florence, Neb.	1862 July 14	Ola N. Liljenquist	250	40	Sept. 23
Florence, Neb.	1862 July 22	Homer Duncan	500	60	Sept. 24
Florence, Neb.	1862 July 28	John R. Murdock	700	65	October
Florence, Neb.	1862 July 28	James S. Brown	200	46	Oct. 2
Florence, Neb.	1862 July 29	Joseph Horne	570	52	Oct. 1

*Number of handcarts

L. D. S. CHURCH IMMIGRATION TO UTAH
Organized Companies Overland

Outfitting Station	Date of Departure	Captain of Company	Persons	Wagons	Arrival in Great Salt Lake Valley
Florence, Neb.	1862 July 30	Isaac Canfield	120	abt. 20	Oct. 16
Florence, Neb.	1862 August	Ancel P. Harmon	500	abt. 60	Oct. 5
Florence, Neb.	1862 Aug. 8	Henry W. Miller	665	60	Oct. 17
Florence, Neb.	1862 August	Horton D. Haight	650	abt. 60	Oct. 19
Florence, Neb.	1862 Aug. 14	William H. Dame	150	50	Oct. 29
Florence, Neb.	1863 June 29	John R. Murdock	275	50	Aug. 29
Florence, Neb.	1863 July 6	John F. Sanders	abt. 250	40	Sept. 5
Florence, Neb.	1863 June 30	A. H. Patterson	200	50	Sept. 4
Florence, Neb.	1863 July 6	John R. Young	abt. 200	44	Sept. 12
Florence, Neb.	1863 July 9	Wm. B. Preston	300	55	Sept. 10
Florence, Neb.	1863 July 25	Peter Nebeker	500	70	Sept. 25
Florence, Neb.	1863 Aug. 6	Daniel D. McArthur	500	75	Oct. 3
Florence, Neb.	1863 Aug. 6	Horton D. Haight	200	abt. 30	Oct. 4
Florence, Neb.	1863 Aug. 9	John W. Woolley	200	30	Oct. 4
Florence, Neb.	1863 Aug. 10	Thomas E. Ricks	400	abt. 60	Oct. 4
Florence, Neb.	1863 Aug. 11	Rosel Hyde	300	abt. 40	Oct. 13
Florence, Neb.	1863 Aug. 14	Samuel White	300	abt. 40	Oct. 15
Wyoming, Neb.	1864 June 25	John D. Chase	85	28	Sept. 20
Wyoming, Neb.	1864 June 29	John R. Murdock	78	abt. 30	Aug. 26
Wyoming, Neb.	1864 July 8	Wm. B. Preston	400	50	Sept. 15
Wyoming, Neb.	1864 July 15	Joseph S. Rawlins	400	50	Sept. 20
Wyoming, Neb.	1864 July	John Smith	abt. 150	20	Oct. 1
Wyoming, Neb.	1864 July 19	Wm. S. Warren	400	abt. 65	Oct. 4
Wyoming, Neb.	1864 July 27	Isaac A. Canfield	211	abt. 50	Oct. 5
Wyoming, Neb.	1864 Aug. 9	Wm. Hyde	350	62	Oct. 26
Wyoming, Neb.	1864 August	Warren S. Snow	abt. 400	abt. 62	Nov. 2
Wyoming, Neb.	1865 July 31	Miner G. Atwood	400	45	Nov. 8
Wyoming, Neb.	1865 Aug. 12	Henson Walker	200	abt. 50	Nov. 9
Wyoming, Neb.	1865 Aug. 12	Wm. W. Willis	200	abt. 50	Nov. 29
Wyoming, Neb.	1866 July 6	Thomas E. Ricks	251	46	Sept. 4
Wyoming, Neb.	1866 July 7	Samuel D. White	230	46	Sept. 5
Wyoming, Neb.	1866 July 13	Wm. Henry Chipman	375	abt. 60	Sept. 15
Wyoming, Neb.	1866 July 19	John D. Holladay	350	69	Sept. 25
Wyoming, Neb.	1866 Aug. 4	Peter Nebeker	400	62	Sept. 29
Wyoming, Neb.	1866 July 25	Daniel Thompson	500	85	Sept. 29
Wyoming, Neb.	1866 Aug. 2	Joseph S. Rawlins	400	65	Oct. 1
Wyoming, Neb.	1866 Aug. 8	Andrew H. Scott	300	49	Oct. 8
Wyoming, Neb.	1866 August	Horton D. Haight (Brought telegraph wire)	abt. 20	65	Oct. 15
Wyoming, Neb.	1866 Aug. 8	Abner Lowry	300	49	Oct. 22
North Platte	1867 Aug. 8	Leonard G. Rice	abt. 500	abt. 50	October
Laramie City, Wyo.	1868 July 25	Chester Loveland	400	40	Aug. 20
Laramie City, Wyo.	1868 July 25	Joseph S. Rawlins	300	31	Aug. 20
Laramie City, Wyo.	1868 July 27	John R. Murdock	600	50	Aug. 19
Laramie City, Wyo.	1868 July 27	Horton D. Haight	275	abt. 30	Aug. 19
Laramie City, Wyo.	1868 Aug. 1	Wm. S. Seeley	272	39	Aug. 29
Benton, Wyoming	1868 Aug. 13	Simpson A. Molen	300	61	Sept. 2
Benton, Wyoming	1868 Aug. 14	Daniel D. McArthur	411	51	Sept. 2
Benton, Wyoming	1868 Aug. 24	John Gillespie	500	50	Sept. 15
Benton, Wyoming	1868 Aug. 31	John G. Holman	650	abt. 90	Sept. 25
Benton, Wyoming	1868 Sept. 1	Edward T. Mumford	250	28	Sept. 24

L.D.S. CHURCH EMIGRATION FROM EUROPE[5]

Date of Sailing	Port of Sailing	Name of Ship	Leader of Company	No. of Persons	Place of Landing
June 6, 1840	Liverpool	Brittania	John Moon	41	New York
Sept. 8, 1840	Liverpool	North America	Theodore Turley	200	New York
Oct. 15, 1840	Liverpool	Isaac Newton	Sam Mulliner	50	New Orleans
Feb. 7, 1841	Liverpool	Sheffield	Hiram Clark	235	New Orleans
Feb. 1841	Bristol	Miscellaneous	Miscellaneous	181	
Feb. 16, 1841	Liverpool	Echo	Daniel Browett	109	New Orleans
Mar. 17, 1841	Liverpool	Uleste (Alesto?)	Thomas Smith	54	New Orleans
Apr. 21, 1841	Liverpool	Rochester	Brigham Young	130	New York
Aug. 8, 1841	Bristol		Thos. Richardson	100	Quebec
Sept. 21, 1841	Liverpool	Tyrean	Joseph Fielding	207	New Orleans
Nov. 8, 1841	Liverpool	Chaos	Peter Melling	170	New Orleans
Jan. 12, 1842	Liverpool	Tremont		143	New Orleans
Feb. 5, 1842	Liverpool	Hope		270	New Orleans
Feb. 20, 1842	Liverpool	John Cummins		200	New Orleans
Mar. 12, 1842	Liverpool	Hanover	Amos Fielding	200	New Orleans
Sept. 17, 1842	Liverpool	Sidney	Levi Richards	180	New Orleans
Sept. 25, 1842	Liverpool	Medford	Orson Hyde	214	New Orleans
Sept. 29, 1842	Liverpool	Henry	John Snider	157	New Orleans
Oct. 29, 1842	Liverpool	Emerald	Parley P. Pratt	250	New Orleans
Jan. 16, 1843	Liverpool	Swanton	Lorenzo Snow	212	New Orleans
Mar. 8, 1843	Liverpool	Yorkshire	Thomas Bullock	83	New Orleans
Mar. 21, 1843	Liverpool	Claiborne		106	New Orleans
Sept. 5, 1843	Liverpool	Metoka		280	New Orleans
Oct. 21, 1843	Liverpool	Champion		91	New Orleans
Jan. 23, 1844	Liverpool	Fanny	William Kay	210	New Orleans
Feb. 6, 1844	Liverpool	Isaac Allerton		60	New Orleans
Feb. 11, 1844	Liverpool	Swanton		81	New Orleans
Mar. 5, 1844	Liverpool	Glasgow	Hiram Clark	150	New Orleans
Sept. 19, 1844	Liverpool	Norfolk		143	New Orleans
Jan. 17, 1845	Liverpool	Palmyra	Amos Fielding	200-?	New Orleans
Feb. 1845	Liverpool			86-?	New Orleans
Sept. 1845	Liverpool	Oregon		125-?	New Orleans
Jan. 16, 1846	Liverpool	Liverpool	Hiram Clark	45	New Orleans
Miscellaneous	Liverpool	Miscellaneous		137	New Orleans
Feb. 20, 1848	Liverpool	Carnatic	F. D. Richards	120	New Orleans
Mar. 9, 1848	Liverpool	Sailor Prince	Moses Martin	80	New Orleans
Sept. 7, 1848	Liverpool	Erin's Queen	Simeon Carter	232	New Orleans
Sept. 24, 1848	Liverpool	Sailor Prince	L. D. Butler	311	New Orleans
Nov. 1848	Liverpool	Lord Sandon		11	New Orleans

Opening of L.D.S. Church, Liverpool Agency Emigration Office, 1849

Date of Sailing	Port of Sailing	Name of Ship	Leader of Company	No. of Persons	Place of Landing
Jan. 29, 1849	Liverpool	Zetland	Orson Spencer	358	New Orleans
Feb. 6, 1849	Liverpool	Ashland	John Johnson	187	New Orleans
Feb. 7, 1849	Liverpool	Henry Ware	Robert Martin	225	New Orleans
Feb. 25, 1849	Liverpool	Buena Vista	Dan Jones	249	New Orleans
Mar. 5, 1849	Liverpool	Hartley	William Hulme	220	New Orleans
Mar. 12, 1849	Liverpool	Emblem	Robert Deans	100	New Orleans
Sept. 2, 1849	Liverpool	James Pennell	Thomas Clark	236	New Orleans
Sept. 5, 1849	Liverpool	Berlin	Jas. G. Brown	253	New Orleans
Nov. 10, 1849	Liverpool	Zetland	S. H. Hawkins	250	New Orleans
Jan. 10, 1850	Liverpool	Argo	Jeter Clinton	402	New Orleans
Feb. 18, 1850	Liverpool	Josiah Bradlee	Thomas Day	263	New Orleans
Mar. 2, 1850	Liverpool	Hartley	David Cook	109	New Orleans

---

[5]Ibid., pp. 147-150.

L.D.S. CHURCH EMIGRATION FROM EUROPE

Date of Sailing	Port of Sailing	Name of Ship	Leader of Company	No. of Persons	Place of Landing
Sept. 4, 1850	Liverpool	North Atlantic	David Sudworth	357	New Orleans
Oct. 2, 1850	Liverpool	James Pennell		254	New Orleans
Oct. 17, 1850	Liverpool	Joseph Badger	John Morris	227	New Orleans
Jan. 6 or 8, 1851	Liverpool	Ellen	J. W. Cummings	466	New Orleans
Jan. 22 or 29, 1851	Liverpool	G. W. Bourne	Wm. Gibson	281	New Orleans
Feb. 1, 1851	Liverpool	Ellen Maria	Geo. D. Watt	378	New Orleans
Mar. 4, 1851	Liverpool	Olympus	Wm. Howell	245	New Orleans
Jan. 10, 1852	Liverpool	Kennebec	John S. Higbee	333	New Orleans
Feb. 10, 1852	Liverpool	Ellen Maria	Isaac C. Haight	369	New Orleans
Mar. 6, 1852	Liverpool	Rockaway		30	New Orleans
Mar. 11, 1852	Liverpool	Italy	O. U. C. Monster	28	New Orleans
Jan. 16, 1853	Liverpool	Forest Monarch	John E. Forsgren	297	New Orleans
Jan. 17, 1853	Liverpool	Ellen Maria	Moses Clawson	332	New Orleans
Jan. 23, 1853	Liverpool	Golconda	Jacob Gates	321	New Orleans
Feb. 5, 1853	Liverpool	Jersey	Geo. Halliday	314	New Orleans
Feb. 15, 1853	Liverpool	Elvira Owen	J. W. Young	345	New Orleans
Feb. 28, 1853	Liverpool	International	Chr. Arthur	425	New Orleans
Feb. 28, 1853	Liverpool	Falcon	Cor. Bagnall	324	New Orleans
Apr. 6, 1853	Liverpool	Camillus	C. E. Bolton	228	New Orleans
Aug. 24, 1853	Liverpool	Page	Bender	17	New Orleans
1853	Liverpool	Misc. Ships	Miscellaneous	23	New Orleans
Jan. 3, 1854	Liverpool	Jesse Munn	Chr. J. Larsen	333	New Orleans
Jan. 22, 1854	Liverpool	Benjamin Adams	H. P. Olsen	384	New Orleans
Feb. 4, 1854	Liverpool	Golconda	Dorr P. Curtis	464	New Orleans
Feb. 22, 1854	Liverpool	Windermere	Daniel Garn	477	New Orleans
Mar. 5, 1854	Liverpool	Old England	John O. Angus	45	New Orleans
Mar. 12, 1854	Liverpool	John M. Wood	Robert Campbell	393	New Orleans
Apr. 4, 1854	Liverpool	Germanicus	Richard Cook	220	New Orleans
Apr. 8, 1854	Liverpool	Marsfield	William Taylor	366	New Orleans
Apr. 24, 1854	Liverpool	Clara Wheeler		29	New Orleans
	Liverpool	Miscellaneous	Miscellaneous	34	New Orleans
Nov. 27, 1854	Liverpool	Clara Wheeler	Henry E. Phelps	422	New Orleans
Jan. 6, 1855	Liverpool	Rockaway	Samuel Glasgow	24	New Orleans
Jan. 7, 1855	Liverpool	James Nesmith	Peter O. Hansen	440	New Orleans
Jan. 9, 1855	Liverpool	Neva	Thomas Jackson	13	New Orleans
Jan. 17, 1855	Liverpool	Charles Buck	Richard Ballantyne	403	New Orleans
Feb. 3, 1855	Liverpool	Isaac Jeans	George C. Riser	16	Philadelphia
Feb. 27, 1855	Liverpool	Siddons	John S. Fullmer	430	Philadelphia
Mar. 31, 1855	Liverpool	Juventa	William Glover	573	Philadelphia
Apr. 17, 1855	Liverpool	Chimborazo	Edward Stevenson	431	Philadelphia
Apr. 22, 1855	Liverpool	Samuel Curling	Israel Barlow	581	New York
Apr. 26, 1855	Liverpool	Wm. Stetson	Aaron Smethurst	293	New York
July 29, 1855	Liverpool	Cynosure	George Seager	159	New York
Nov. 30, 1855	Liverpool	Emerald Isle	Phil C. Merrill	350	New York
Dec. 12, 1855	Liverpool	John J. Boyd	Knud Peterson	512	New York
Miscellaneous	Liverpool	Miscellaneous	Miscellaneous	319	Mis.
Feb. 18, 1856	Liverpool	Caravan	Daniel Tyler	457	New York
Mar. 23, 1856	Liverpool	Enoch Train	James Ferguson	534	Boston
Apr. 19, 1856	Liverpool	Samuel Curling	Dan Jones	707	Boston
May 4, 1856	Liverpool	Thornton	James G. Willie	764	New York
May 25, 1856	Liverpool	Horizon	Edward Martin	856	Boston
June 1, 1856	Liverpool	Wellfleet	John Aubray	146	Boston
Nov. 18, 1856	Liverpool	Columbia	J. Williams	223	New York
Miscellaneous	Liverpool	Miscellaneous		69	

L.D.S. CHURCH EMIGRATION FROM EUROPE

Date of Sailing	Port of Sailing	Name of Ship	Leader of Company	No. of Persons	Place of Landing
Mar. 28, 1857	Liverpool	Geo. Washington	J. P. Park	817	Boston
Apr. 25, 1857	Liverpool	Westmoreland	Mathew Cowley	544	Philadelphia
May 30, 1857	Liverpool	Tuscarora	Richard Harper	547	Philadelphia
July 18, 1857	Liverpool	Wyoming	Chas. Harmon	36	Philadelphia
Miscellaneous	Liverpool	Miscellaneous		30	
Jan. 21, 1858	Liverpool	Underwriter	Henry Harriman	25	New York
Feb. 19, 1858	Liverpool	Empire	Jesse Hobson	64	New York
Mar. 22, 1858	Liverpool	John Bright	Iver N. Iversen	90	New York
Apr. 11, 1859	Liverpool	Wm. Tappscott	Robert F. Neslen	725	New York
July 10, 1859	Liverpool	Antarctic	James Chaplow	30	New York
Aug. 20, 1859	Liverpool	Emerald Isle	Henry Hug	54	New York
Mar. 30, 1860	Liverpool	Underwriter	James D. Ross	594	New York
May 11, 1860	Liverpool	Wm. Tappscott	Asa Calkin	731	New York
	Liverpool	Miscellaneous		84	
Apr. 16, 1861	Liverpool	Manchester	C. V. Spencer	380	New York
Apr. 23, 1861	Liverpool	Underwriter	Milo Andrus	624	New York
May 16, 1861	Liverpool	Monarch of the Sea	Jabez Woodard	955	New York
Apr. 9, 1862	Hamburg	Humboldt	H. C. Hansen	323	New York
Apr. 15, 1862	Hamburg	Franklin	Chr. A. Madsen	413	New York
Apr. 18, 1862	Hamburg	Electric	Soren Christoffersen	336	New York
Apr. 23, 1862	Liverpool	John J. Boyd	J. S. Brown	701	New York
Apr. 25, 1862	Hamburg	Athenia	Ola N. Liljenquist	484	New York
May 6, 1862	Liverpool	Manchester	J. D. T. McAllister	376	New York
May 14, 1862	Liverpool	Wm. Tappscott	Wm. Gibson	808	New York
May 15, 1862	Havre	Windermere	S. L. Ballif	110	New York
May 18, 1862	Liverpool	Antarctic	W. C. Moody	38	New York
Miscellaneous	Liverpool	Miscellaneous		8	
Apr. 30, 1863	Liverpool	John J. Boyd	Wm. W. Cluff	763	New York
May 8, 1863	Liverpool	B. S. Kimball	H. P. Lund	654	New York
May 8, 1863	Liverpool	Consignment	A. Christensen	38	New York
May 23, 1863	Liverpool	Antarctic	J. Needham	483	New York
May 30, 1863	Liverpool	Cynosure	D. M. Stuart	754	New York
June 4, 1863	London	Amazon	Wm. Bramall	882	New York
Miscellaneous	Liverpool	Miscellaneous		72	
Apr. 28, 1864	Liverpool	Monarch of the Sea	John Smith	974	New York
May 21, 1864	Liverpool	Gen. McClellan	Thos. E. Jeremy	802	New York
June 3, 1864	London	Hudson	John M. Kay	863	New York
Miscellaneous	Liverpool	Miscellaneous		58	
Apr. 29, 1865	Liverpool	Belle Wood	Wm. H. Shearman	636	New York
May 8, 1865	Hamburg	B. S. Kimball	A. W. Winberg	558	New York
May 10, 1865	Liverpool	D. Hoadley	Wm. Underwood	24	New York
Miscellaneous	Liverpool	Miscellaneous		83	
Apr. 30, 1866	Liverpool	John Bright	C. M. Gillett	747	New York
May 5, 1866	London	Caroline	S. H. Hill	389	New York
May 23, 1866	London	Am. Congress	John Nicholson	350	New York
May 25, 1866	Hamburg	Kenilworth	Sam L. Sprague	684	New York
May 30, 1866	Liverpool	Arkwright	J. C. Wixom	450	New York
May 30, 1866	London	C. Grinnell	R. Harrison	26	New York
June 1, 1866	Hamburg	Cavour	N. Nielsen	201	New York
June 2, 1866	Hamburg	Humboldt	Geo. M. Brown	328	New York
June 6, 1866	Liverpool	Saint Mark	A. Stevens	104	New York
Miscellaneous	Liverpool	Miscellaneous		56	
June 21, 1867	Liverpool	Manhattan	Arch N. Hill	482	New York

L.D.S. CHURCH EMIGRATION FROM EUROPE

Date of Sailing	Port of Sailing	Name of Ship	Leader of Company	No. of Persons	Place of Landing
Miscellaneous	Liverpool	Miscellaneous		178	
June 4, 1868	Liverpool	John Bright	James McGaw	722	New York
June 20, 1868	Liverpool	Emerald Isle	H. Jensen Hals	876	New York
June 24, 1868	Liverpool	Constitution	Harvey H. Cluff	457	New York
June 30, 1868	Liverpool	Minnesota	John Parry	534	New York
July 14, 1868	Liverpool	Colorado	Wm. B. Preston	600	New York
Miscellaneous	Liverpool	Miscellaneous		43	

UTAH IMMIGRATION CARD INDEX

Time Period: 1847-1868.

Origin and Contents: The Utah Immigration Card Index (variously referred to as Crossing the Plains Card Catalogue, Crossing the Plains Card Index, Crossing the Plains, Pioneer Card Catalogue, Emigrations Crossing the Plains, and Company List Index) is an index of names of pioneer immigrants to Utah. Names included in the index are of emigrants from foreign countries as well as natives of the United States. The data in the card index has been compiled from various sources including the *Journal History of The Church of Jesus Christ of Latter-day Saints* (*Journal History*) (See Chapter 18.), "Deseret News," *Pioneers and Prominent Men of Utah,*[6] and *Church Chronology.*[7] None of these sources appear to have been indexed completely.

The card index is arranged alphabetically by surname, and usually by head of the household; in rare instances cards may be found for each member of a household. (Copies of these cards are available in room 305 of the Church Office Building grouped chronologically by arrival date of each company in Great Salt Lake Valley.) Information on the index cards varies and may include the following:

1. Names (indicated head of household and members of group).

---

[6]Frank Esshom, *Pioneers and Prominent Men of Utah* (Salt Lake City: Utah Pioneers Book Publishing Co., 1913).

[7]Andrew Jenson, *Church Chronology* (Salt Lake City: Deseret News, 1914).

2. Ages.
3. Relationships (rarely mentioned).
4. Date of arrival.
5. Name of pioneer company.
6. Date of departure.
7. Name of ship.
8. Source of information (usually indicated by abbreviations).

> J.H.—*Journal History of The Church of Jesus Christ of Latter-day Saints.*
>
> Supplement—*Supplement to the Journal History of The Church of Jesus Christ of Latter-day Saints.*
>
> Ch. Chr. or Ch. Chron.—*Church Chronology.*[8]
>
> Des. News—*"Deseret News."*

Availability:

1. Microfilmed copy of card index—library of The Genealogical Society.

2. Original index—Church Historian's Office.

Genealogical Application:

1. The Utah Immigration Card Index refers to the original record source where additional information may be recorded. However, most of the information about a person or family was transferred from the source to the index card.

2. Persons whose names are grouped together may be related.

3. The arrival date aids in establishing the period of time to search in local records.

4. Private journals and diaries compiled by members of the same company may contain additional information.

5. Information may be found regarding European emigrants who left their homeland prior to 1849, the year of organization of the L.D.S. Church Emigration Office in Liverpool, England.

---

[8]*Ibid.*

Genealogical Limitations:

1. Cards are usually arranged by head of the household and list only those who traveled in L.D.S. sponsored groups. Some company rosters were lost, and consequently, valuable genealogical information about some pioneer immigrants was not available for indexing.

2. The indicated family groups are not always complete, and relationships are rarely given.

EUROPEAN EMIGRATION CARD INDEX

Time Period: 1849-1925.

Origin and Contents: The European Emigration Card Index (variously referred to as Crossing the Ocean, Emigration Card Catalogue, Shipping File Index, Index to Shipping, etc.) is an index of names of persons who emigrated from European countries. The majority were associated with The Church of Jesus Christ of Latter-day Saints and registered for passage through the L.D.S. Church Liverpool, England Emigration Office. There is some uncertainty as to every source that has been indexed; however, most of the data in the card index has been compiled from information in the *Emigration Registers of the British Mission.* The *Emigration Registers of the Scandinavian Mission, Church Chronology,*[9] *History of the Scandinavian Mission,*[10] "Deseret News," etc., have also been used in compiling the index. The emigration records of the Swedish Mission, Netherlands Mission, and some from the Scandinavian Mission have not been card indexed; however, the names of prospective passengers appearing in the registers of the Netherlands Mission and the Scandinavian Mission, and in the registers of the Swedish Mission through the year 1913 are also recorded in the *Emigration Registers of the British Mission* which has been indexed.

The card index is arranged alphabetically by surname, and usually by name of the head of the household—in some instances by name of the head of a group of friends. On some cards is re-

---

[9]*Ibid.*

[10]Andrew Jenson, *History of the Scandinavian Mission* (Salt Lake City: Deseret News Press, 1927).

corded the name of a single individual who might have been an emigrant or a returning missionary. (Copies of these cards are available in room 305 of the Church Office Building grouped chronologically by departure date of each ship.) Information on the cards varies and may include the following:

1. Names.
2. Number of persons in group.
3. Ages.
4. Nationality, country, or conference.
5. Date of departure.
6. Place of departure (if not listed, probably Liverpool).
7. Name of the ship (e.g., "Caroline," "Minnesota," "Amazon," "Siddons," "Caravan," etc.).
8. Place of arrival.
9. Date of arrival.
10. Source of information (usually indicated by abbreviations).

   B.M.—British Mission

   Lib. Bk., Lib. No., or Lib. Bk. No.—Refers to a library book number (usually an emigration register) in the Church Historian's Office.

   J.H.—*Journal History of The Church of Jesus Christ of Latter-day Saints.*

   Ch. Chr. or Ch. Chron.—*Church Chronology*[11]

   Hist. of the Scand. Miss.—*History of the Scandinavian Mission.*[12]

   Des. News—"Deseret News"

Availability:

1. Microfilmed copy of card index—library of The Genealogical Society.

2. Original index—Church Historian's Office.

Genealogical Application:

1. The European Emigration Card Index refers to the original record source where additional information may be recorded.

---

[11]Andrew Jenson, *Church Chronology*, op. cit.
[12]Andrew Jenson, *History of the Scandinavian Mission*, op. cit.

2. The card index establishes a departure date and can be used as an aid to find names in some unindexed L.D.S. emigration registers. Some names were recorded in more than one register concurrently, and the information differs. Names of prospective passengers in Continental European registers were often repeated in those of the British Mission, and those of the British Mission may appear in more than one register of that mission.

Genealogical Limitations:

1. Cards are usually arranged by the head of the household and list only those who traveled in L.D.S. Church sponsored groups. Index cards were not compiled from all L.D.S. Church emigration registers, and some registers were only partially indexed.

EMIGRATION REGISTERS OF THE BRITISH MISSION

Time Period: 1849-1885; 1899-1925.

Origin: The *Emigration Registers of the British Mission* (variously referred to as Shipping Records, Emigrations by Ship; Passenger Lists; Emigration Records of the British Mission; and Liverpool Office Emigration Records) were compiled by the L.D.S. Church agent at the Liverpool, England Emigration Office. Passage for L.D.S. Church sponsored emigrants from the British Isles and Continental Europe was usually arranged and coordinated through this office.

Frequently British Mission registers were kept concurrently and the names of the same persons repeated; sometimes additional information is given. When this occurred, usually only one of these registers was indexed in the European Emigration Card Index.

Contents: The passenger information in each register is recorded with the name of the ship on which the passenger was assigned to sail; these ships are usually listed chronologically by departure date. The destination, or port of debarkation, is usually listed. Names of passengers from Continental Europe (Scandinavia, Italy, France, Poland, Germany, Holland, Belgium, and Switzerland), Australia, and South Africa may or may not be listed; when they are listed, the names of these passengers are usually grouped together immediately following British Isles passengers and are listed under the name of the appropriate mission or nationality. Information on prospective passengers varies and may include the following:

1. Ticket no.
2. Names (includes those who sailed, as well as those who applied for passage and withdrew).
3. Date of initial deposit.
4. Married or single.
5. Age.
6. Sex.
7. Occupation.
8. Address or residence.
9. "C" (country or nationality).
10. Settlement (amount paid).
11. Description of emigrant (Describes financial means: Ordinary—passenger paid regular or ordinary fare and was responsible for purchasing own supplies at outfitting stations in the United States; P.E. Fund—Loan from Perpetual Emigrating Fund Company; £10 Company; £13 Company; etc.—passage and supplies furnished for set fee).
12. Notification of date of sailing.
13. Conference.
14. Relationships (rarely mentioned).
15. The name of the President of the Company is often recorded, and is usually found at the end of the list of passengers assigned to sail on a particular ship.

Availabiliy:
1. Microfilmed copy—library of The Genealogical Society.
2. Original—Church Historian's Office.

The *Emigration Registers of the British Mission* have been microfilmed with several registers per microfilm. Listed below are the call numbers at the library of The Genealogical Society, the library book numbers of these registers in the Church Historian's Office, and the years each register covers.

Gen. Soc. Call No. Serial No.	Part No.	C.H.O. Lib. Bk. No.	Years Covered
6184	1	1043	1849-1851
		1044	1851-1855
		1040	1854-1855
6184	2	1045	1855-1856
		1046	1856-1860
		1047	1861-1863
6184	3	1048	1863-1868
		1049	1868
		1041	1868-1874
6184	4	1042	1875-1885
		1825	1899-1903
		3067	1901-1913
6184	5	1826	1903-1906
		1827	1905-1909
		1828	1909-1914
		1829	1910-1914
6184	6	3312	1913-1919
		3311	1914-1924
		3313	1914-1925
		3310	1910-1923*

*(a statistical report, no names of persons)

Genealogical Application:

1. The persons whose names are grouped together or who are from the same conference (district) may be related.

2. The information may be from a primary source. These registers often contain information a person gave about himself.

3. The ticket number indicates persons traveling together—often they are members of the same family.

4. The age at a dated event is an aid in calculating a birth year.

5. The occupations are clues to identity and may lead to occupational trade or gild (guild) records.

6. The address and/or local residence indicates the geographic locality for records to search in the foreign country in the research phase.

7. The departure date aids in establishing the period of time to be searched in records of the United States and the foreign country.

8. The name of the port of arrival indicates likely places of temporary or permanent settlement.

9. Names of some persons who did not sail are included in the *Emigration Registers of the British Mission* but not in the index.

Genealogical Limitations:

1. The indicated family groups are not always complete and relationships are rarely given.

2. The names of passengers from Continental European countries may or may not be listed in the *Emigration Registers of the British Mission.*

3. Some registers are not indexed.

4. L.D.S. Church emigrants traveling independently were not registered through the Liverpool office.

5. The address or residence may or may not be the home address, but rather an address of lodging for a night or temporary period of time prior to sailing.

6. The records from 1886-1898 are missing.

EMIGRATION REGISTERS OF CONTINENTAL EUROPE

Origin: These registers (also referred to as Shipping Records, Emigration by Ship; Passenger Lists; and Emigration Records) are registers of names of persons for whom arrangements were made for emigrating from various countries to the United States (usually via Liverpool, England) by registering with L.D.S. authorities of their respective missions. Often these authorities then coordinated with the L.D.S. agent in Liverpool, England, for final arrangements. Index cards have been compiled from some of the registers and are included in the European Emigration Card Index.

Contents: The following emigration registers kept by authorities of The Church of Jesus Christ of Latter-day Saints in Continental Europe contain names of persons from various countries of Europe:

1. Scandinavian Mission—Denmark, Norway, and Sweden.

2. Netherlands Mission—Germany, Switzerland, Belgium, Hungary, Holland, etc.

3. Swedish Mission—Sweden.

Each register contains information on prospective passengers; however, the arrangement of the information and the content of the information varies. Some names are listed under the conference of membership, and others under the name and embarkation date of the ship. Regardless of the format of the registers, the individuals are listed chronologically by sailing date. The information may include the following:

1. Conference.
2. Name of ship.
3. Name of individual.
4. Age.
5. Sex.
6. Residence.
7. Birthplace (sometimes by town; sometimes by country).
8. Occupation.
9. Record of passage.
10. Remarks (often contain genealogical data).
11. Remitter (often a relative).
12. Remitter's address (often Utah or Idaho).
13. Date of sailing.
14. Sailing from.
15. Destination of person.

Availability:
1. Microfilmed copy—library of the Genealogical Society.
2. Original—Church Historian's Office.

Several registers have been included on each roll of microfilm. Listed below are the call numbers at the library of The Genealogical Society, the library book numbers of these registers in the Church Historian's Office, and the years each register covers.

Mission Register	Gen. Soc. Call No. Serial No.	Part No.	CHO Lib. Bk. No.	Years Covered
Scandinavian	6185	1	1203	1853-1866
			1059	1854-1863
			1060	1864-1865
			1061	1866
			1062	1867-1869
			1063	1870-1872
			1064	1873-1881
			1065	1881-1886
	6185	2	23591	1901-1914
			23590	1901-1920
Netherlands	6186	1	4413	1904-1907
			4414	1907-1909
			4415	1909-1911
			4416	1909-1914
Swedish	6188		23529	1905-1932

Genealogical Application:

1. Though some of these registers have not been indexed, the European Emigration Card Index should be searched to establish the departure date as names of persons appearing in L.D.S. Church registers of the Swedish Mission prior to December 31, 1913, and L.D.S. Church registers of the Netherlands Mission and Scandinavian Mission often were recorded also in the *Emigration Registers of the British Mission* which were indexed.

2. Persons whose names are grouped together or who are from the same locality may be related.

3. The information may be from a primary source. These registers often contain information a person gave about himself or members of his family.

4. An age at a dated event is an aid in calculating a birth year.

5. Occupations are clues to identity and may lead to occupational trade or gild (guild) records.

6. The residence indicates the geographic locality for searching records in the foreign country.

7. The departure date aids in establishing the period of time for searching in records of the United States and the foreign country in the survey phase and the research phase.

8. The destination may be a clue to geographic area of settlement.

9. The party requesting the reservation (or remitter) of the prospective passenger is often a relative.

Genealogical Limitations:

1. Some registers have not been included in the European Emigration Card Index.

2. Information on indicated family groups may be inaccurate or incomplete.

3. L.D.S. Church emigrants traveling independently were not registered.

4. Registers for some time periods are missing.

PROJECT ASSIGNMENTS

1. Search the following indexes that apply to the family group record selected in Chapter 6:
a. Utah Immigration Card Index.
b. European Emigration Card Index.

2. Search the emigration registers as indicated on the index cards.

SUGGESTED READING

"They Came In 1847," *Daughters of Utah Pioneers*, Salt Lake City, 1947, pp. 401-448. Lists of pioneers immigrating to Great Salt Lake Valley in 1847. Names of immigrating companies arranged chronologically by arrival date. Information under name of company may include the following: name of pioneer, his age, birth date and place, and death date and place. (Contains information similar to that in two manuscripts in the

Church Historian's Office: *Utah Pioneers of 1847*, and *The Mormon Battalion*.)

"They Came in 1848," *Daughters of Utah Pioneers*, Salt Lake City, 1948, pp. 453-521. List of names of pioneers to Great Salt Lake Valley in 1848, arranged alphabetically by surname, and may include age, and date and place of birth.

"They Came in 1849," *Daughters of Utah Pioneers*, Salt Lake City, 1949, pp. 429-472. List of names of pioneers to Great Salt Lake Valley in 1849, arranged alphabetically by surname, and may include age, and date and place of birth.

"They Came in 1850," *Daughters of Utah Pioneers*, Salt Lake City, 1950. pp. 377-455. List of names of pioneers to Great Salt Lake Valley in 1850, arranged alphabetically by surname, and may include age, and date and place of birth.

Hafen, LeRoy R., and Hafen, Ann. *Handcarts to Zion*. Glendale, California: Arthur H. Clark Co., 1960. An account of the ten handcart companies, 1856-1860; journals, reports, and rosters of the companies.

Perpetual Emigrating Fund Co. *Names of Persons and Sureties Indebted to the Perpetual Emigrating Fund Company from 1850 to 1877 Inclusive*. Salt Lake City: Star Book and Job Printing Office, 1877. Names of persons who immigrated to Great Salt Lake Valley from various parts of the United States and from foreign countries with financial aid from the P. E. Fund Co.; gives arrival date.

Tyler, Daniel. *A Concise History of the Mormon Battalion in the Mexican War, 1846-1847*. Chicago, Rio Grande Press Inc., 1964. Reprint of the 1881 edition; information is taken from private journals, diaries, etc.

Chapter Sixteen

L.D.S. CHURCH RECORDS
OF MEMBERSHIP

The records initiated by The Church of Jesus Christ of Latter-day Saints can be classified as Historical Records and Records of Membership. (See Chapter 18 for Historical Records.)

ORIGIN

Records of members of The Church of Jesus Christ of Latter-day Saints were kept from the time of the organization of The Church in 1830; but many of the early ones have been lost or destroyed. The majority of the membership records which originated in wards (branches) in the United States prior to 1850 are missing.

Some of the first records of membership were recorded on loose sheets of paper, in notebooks, and with no uniform format. Often records of members were combined with historical records which contain minutes of meetings and/or other types of historical information, or anything the ward (branch) clerk felt was important. Sometimes the recorded information is very sparse, sometimes quite complete, and often in chronological order as the events occurred.

After 1877, frequently more than one membership record book was kept concurrently in each ward, e.g., records of members and records of baptisms were kept in one book; records of children, births, and blessings in another; and records of priesthood ordinations in another. Sometimes these events were recorded in the same book; but divisions were made in the book and events recorded chronologically by date in the respective divisions. Indexes were kept up to date and arranged alphabetically by the first letter of the individual's surname.

After 1877, notices were issued intermittently from the General Authorities giving specific instructions concerning types of books and forms to be used and information to be recorded. Some ward (branch) clerks did not conform to the recommended instructions; some may not have received the instructions, or they received instructions some time after they were to become effective. The books and forms that were recommended were not printed by one publishing company nor distributed throughout The Church from one distribution center. The books and forms were printed locally, resulting in slight variations as to format from locality to locality; but, information requested on the forms or in the books is similar.

Even though certain types of books were recommended for the keeping of records, if a ward (branch) clerk still had a good supply of unused pages in his record book, frequently he filled that book before beginning the new recommended book. At other times when the clerks were instructed to forward their records to the Church Historian's Office, they were reluctant to do so; many never did. Some clerks were careless with their records so that they were destroyed or lost, and some records were unavoidably destroyed by fire, etc. (Old record books thought to have been lost or destroyed are constantly being discovered and deposited with the Church Historian.) Other ward (branch) clerks copied information from the original record book into one of the same type or one of a newer recommended type, forwarded the copy to the Church Historian's Office, and kept the original in the ward (branch), thus accounting for an event which occurred in 1910 being recorded in a record book that was not recommended until 1920.

Prior to 1941, as Church members moved from one ward to another, it was the responsibility of each family to obtain a letter or statement from their present ward (branch) clerk to be delivered to the ward (branch) clerk where the family was moving, giving details of membership in the Church, including baptism, priesthood ordinations, vital data, etc. Often the previous ward clerk did not give a full account of all events or vital data pertaining to the family members, and sometimes he did not extract the information from his ward (branch) records, but recorded information from oral statements given by the family or member at the time the letter of recommendation was being compiled. Many times a family that was moving did not bother to get a letter or statement of recommendation from the ward clerk; names of inactive members may never have been recorded by the clerk.

Since 1941, a separate form for a record of membership has been kept for each person. When an individual moves from one ward to another, the ward clerk forwards the membership form to the Presiding Bishop's Office where it is forwarded to the new ward of residence. This prevents duplication of membership and establishes a more efficient method of transferring records of members from one ward to another.

CONTENTS

Many of the early branch membership records, and particularly those of foreign missions, vary considerably from ward records as to format. Some of the particular record books recommended for use in the wards were never introduced in the branches, and others that were recommended for use in the wards were not used in the branches until some years later. Some wards were slow in adopting the recommended forms.

Prior to 1877: Ward membership records prior to 1877 usually were not indexed; entries were arranged chronologically. The records were kept in various types of ledgers, registers, and notebooks as the Church had not established a standard format. Often histories of the ward, minutes of meetings, and blessings, baptisms, confirmations, ordinations, etc., were combined with records of memberships

The record of membership is usually a one-line entry, sometimes containing only the name of the member, and at other times, birth date and place, parentage (including mother's maiden surname), date of baptism and by whom, and date of confirmation and by whom. There are often various records of ordinations to the priesthood.

  1877-1900: The first standardized form to be used for records of membership in the wards of the Church was introduced in 1877 in what is often called the "long book" or "large book" as it is about four feet long when open. (These books were not used in the branches of the missions.) There is an index to the names of members at the beginning of the book; it is arranged alphabetically by first letter of the surname and the reference number refers to the membership record number rather than a page number. The membership record numbers are arranged consecutively in the main part of the book. The heading on the pages of the main part of the record book is printed across the top of two pages and reads, "Record of Members of The Church of Jesus Christ of Latter-day Saints of .... Ward, ... Stake of Zion." Ward clerks were instructed to record the names of all current members of the ward in the new book. Each record of membership is a one-line entry extending across two pages, and the information called for includes the following:

1. Membership record number.
2. Name of individual.
3. Father's name.
4. Mother's maiden name.
5. Birth date and place.
6. Blessing date and by whom.
7. First baptism date and by whom.
8. First confirmation date and by whom.
9. Ordination date, to what office, and by whom.
10. Rebaptism date and by whom.
11. Reconfirmation date and by whom.
12. Date received into ward and where from.

13. Date removed from ward and where moving to.
14. Death date.
15. Remarks.

Some ward clerks kept additional books concurrently, e.g., records of births and blessings of children.

1900-1920: On March 22, 1900 a smaller-sized membership book was recommended for general use throughout The Church; this book has an index and three additional parts.

Index: The index is referred to as a triple index as there are references to the three parts of the book. The names in the index are arranged alphabetically by the first letter of the surname, and all reference numbers refer to the membership record numbers in the respective parts of the book rather than page numbers.

Part I: Part I is titled, "Record of Members of The Church of Jesus Christ of Latter-day Saints." The names of individuals who presently resided in the ward were recorded first. Names of new members were added chronologically. When members died, moved from the ward, or were excommunicated, an X was written in the column immediately preceding the name, and a note of the cause inserted in the "Remarks" column. In all instances where information about members was continued in Part II, "Records of Ordinations," the proper entry was recorded in the last column in Part I headed "Continued in Record of Ordination No." Information requested in Part I is as follows:

1. Membership record number.
2. Name of individual.
3. Father's name.
4. Mother's maiden name.
5. Birth date and place.
6. Baptism date and by whom.
7. Confirmation date and by whom.

Part II: Part II is titled, "Record of Ordinations to the Priesthood." Names in this part are repeated from Part I, "Record of Members." Not only were all the ordinations that took place in the ward recorded in Part II, but ordinations performed in wards of previous residence could also be entered, provided the proper certificates were shown to the ward clerk to prove such ordinations. Dates of ordinations were not to be supplied from memory.

When a person was advanced in the priesthood, an X was written in the column immediately preceding the name, and a note inserted in the "Remarks" column giving the new number where the name was re-entered. In case of removal, death, excommunication, etc., the X was also written in the column designated for that purpose, and the cause in the "Remarks" column.

The following information is requested in Part II:

1. Record of ordination number.
2. Record of member number continued from.
3. Name of individual.
4. Date of ordination, to what office, and by whom.
5. Remarks.

Part III: Part III is titled, "Record of Children Under 8 Years of Age and Not Baptized." Names of children presently living in the ward were entered in this record in alphabetical order by surname. As babies were born or blessed, or children received from other wards, their names were entered chronologically. When a child died or moved from the ward or the name was transferred to Part I, "Record of Members" (which was done when a child was baptized) an X was written in the column immediately preceding the name, and the cause recorded in the "Remarks" column. When a child was baptized and his name transferred to Part I, the number given in Part I was written in Part III in the column headed "Transferred to Record of Members, No." Information called for in Part III follows:

1. Record of child number.
2. Name of child.
3. Date and place of birth.
4. Father's name.
5. Mother's maiden name.
6. Date of blessing and by whom.

7. Remarks.

8. Transferred to Record of Members No.

1907-Present: The Form E was introduced in 1907 and is an annual report of certain events involving members of The Church of Jesus Christ of Latter-day Saints, and includes servicemen enlistments, missionary callings, births and blessings, baptisms and confirmations, priesthood ordinations, divorces, excommunications, and deaths. Each event is recorded in the Form E by the ward clerk near the time the event occurs. At the end of each year, the Form E is forwarded to the stake clerk who compiles a statistical summary from the combined Form E reports from wards in his stake, and then forwards the ward Form E reports and the statistical summary to the Presiding Bishop's Office; from there they are forwarded to the Church Historian's Office. From 1908 through 1917 the stake clerk, in addition to compiling a statistical summary, combined the ward Form E reports into a stake Form E report for submission to the Presiding Bishop's Office.

The following information is requested in the Form E; (that which is *underlined* was not requested on the earliest Form E reports):

1. Missionaries: name, sex, priesthood, full time or stake, departure date or date set apart, date released or returned, and name of mission.

2. Marriages: name, sex, priesthood, *date and place of birth,* date and place of marriage, whether the marriage was "Temple," "Church-civil," or "Other-civil," to whom married, and whether or not this person is an L.D.S. Church member.

3. Births and blessings: name, sex, father's name, mother's maiden name, date and place of birth, date blessed and by whom.

4. Baptisms and confirmations: name, sex, *if convert,* father's name, mother's maiden name, date and place of birth, date baptized and by whom, and date confirmed and by whom.

5. Priesthood ordinations: name, *date of birth*, date of ordination, to what office ordained and by whom, former office in the priesthood if any, and if over 21.

6. Deaths: name, sex, priesthood, member or child, *single married, divorced, widow, widower, father's name, mother's maiden name, date and place of birth*, date and *place* of death, cause of death, and *occupation.*

7. Divorces: name, sex, priesthood, *date and place of birth*, date of divorce (to be recorded when divorce is final), kind of marriage—"Temple," "Church-civil," or "Other-civil,"—from whom divorced, and whether or not this person is a member of The Church.

8. Excommunications: name, sex, priesthood, *date and place of birth*, date and cause of excommunication, single, married, widow, widower, divorced.

1920-1941: In 1920 a new book for records of membership was introduced. It includes an index where names are alphabetically arranged by first letter of the surname; the reference number usually refers to a record of membership number. The membership forms are numbered consecutively, and there are 4, 5, or 6 to a page depending on who printed the book. Information requested on the membership forms includes the following:

1. Record of membership number.
2. Name of individual.
3. Father's name.
4. Mother's maiden name.
5. Birth date and place.
6. Blessing date and by whom.
7. Baptism date and by whom.
8. Confirmation date and by whom.
9. Dates of ordination to the priesthood, to what office, and by whom ordained.
10. Date received, and from what ward.
11. Date removed, and to what ward.

12. Missionary information.

13. To whom married and whether marriage was "Temple," or "Civil."

14. Excommunication date.

15. Death date and cause.

Blessings, baptisms, marriages, ordinations, etc., were recorded chronologically in the Form E reports for this period of time.

During 1920-1941, some wards in Granite and Liberty Stakes in Salt Lake City, Utah, kept separate cards for membership rather than the recommended membership book.

1941-Present: In 1941 an 8½" x 5" form for record of membership was introduced which could be kept alphabetically in a loose-leaf type binder. Both a white form and a green form were compiled for each member of the L.D.S. Church by the ward clerk in 1941. As babies have been born into L.D.S. families and as persons previously of other faiths have been baptized, the same procedure has been followed. The white forms are retained by the ward clerk and the green copy is sent to the Presiding Bishop's Office.

When a person leaves his residence temporarily such as to enter the armed forces or college, the white membership record is retained by the ward clerk and a pink duplicate forwarded to the ward of temporary residence. When a person moves permanently from a ward, the clerk forwards the white membership record to the Presiding Bishop's Office for forwarding to the new ward of new residence. Also, when an individual dies, his white membership record is forwarded to the Presiding Bishop's Office.

The green membership forms in the Presiding Bishop's Office are arranged alphabetically and result in a master file of L.D.S. Church records of members. These records of members are kept current as information is transferred from the Form E reports which are received in the Presiding Bishop's Office at the end of each year and as white membership records are received for forwarding to other wards. When a person dies, the white record of membership received in the Presiding Bishop's Office is checked and compared with the green form and brought up to date. The green form is retained, and the white card is forwarded to the Church Historian's Office and placed in the Deceased Members File.

The white records of membership in the Deceased Members File are arranged alphabetically and result in a Church-wide file of names of L.D.S. Church members who have died since 1941.

The information requested on the white, green, and pink cards includes the following:

1. Name of individual.

2. Current address.

3. Father's full name.

4. Mother's full maiden name.

5. Date born.

6. Place born.

7. Citizenship.

8. L.D.S. Church blessing, baptism, priesthood ordination, and marriage data.

9. Missionary data.

10. Name of spouse (and whether member or non-member).

11. Name, birth date and birth place of children and who children married.

12. A ward-to-ward record which includes date moved, to which ward and stake, street and city address, date posted at Presiding Bishop's Office, and date accepted.

13. Name of former spouse and whether deceased or divorced. Date and place of this marriage, and information regarding children of this marriage.

14. Date, place, and cause of death.

15. On earliest individual membership records there is a space to record dependents other than children.

DETERMINING WARD OF RESIDENCE

One must learn the name of the ward (branch) of residence to search membership records prior to 1941. Often a city has more than one ward, or a branch may include members from more than one town. To determine the ward of residence in a large city, one must know the address of the individual about whom information is desired. This address may be obtained from the memory of family members, old letters, city directories, etc. Ward boundaries change from time to time; a helpful reference for establishing boundaries of early wards is the *Encyclopedic History of the Church of Jesus Christ of Latter-day Saints.*[1] There is also a Ward Organization Card File in the Church Historian's Office compiled from the *Encyclopedic History* which is kept current. These two references contain an alphabetical listing of missions, stakes, and wards and branches of stakes, and give their boundaries and dates of organization. A map could be used to outline the ward boundaries for the particular time period to determine the ward in which the particular address was located. *Church Chronology*[2] and the *Journal of The Church of Jesus Christ of Latter-day Saints* (See Chapter 18) may also be helpful in establishing the date of ward organization.

To determine the ward or branch of membership when one ward or branch boundary covered a large area, one should obtain a map and mark the place of residence. Then with a different color pencil, mark the wards or branches in the general area. There is a Register of Contents (*Ward, Branch, and Mission Records of The Church of Jesus Christ of Latter-day Saints up to 1948 [Locality Arrangement]*) available at the library of The Genealogical Society which lists the names of the wards and branches by state and country. It may be necessary to search the membership records of more than one ward or branch.

Membership Card Index: The Membership Card Index to early L.D.S. Church ward and branch membership record books (sometimes referred to as the Partial Card Index or Minnie Margetts' File)

---

[1] Andrew Jenson, *Encyclopedic History of The Church of Jesus Christ of Latter-day Saints* (Salt Lake City: Deseret News Publishing Co.), 1941.

[2] Andrew Jenson, *Church Chronology.* op. cit.

is an index to membership records from over 400 wards and branches, particularly branches of the British Mission. There are three sections in the index: (1) cards listing wards, branches, conferences, and stakes that have been indexed; (2) index cards with incomplete names which are arranged alphabetically according to locality; and (3) index cards, arranged alphabetically by surname of the individual, containing information extracted from the ward and branch records. Cards in sections 2 and 3 may contain the following information:

1. Name of individual.
2. Father's name.
3. Mother's maiden name.
4. When born.
5. Where born.
6. When baptized.
7. Where baptized.
8. By whom baptized.
9. Ward or branch.
10. Stake or mission.
11. Ordination.
12. By whom ordained.
13. Remarks.
14. Record source—book no., page no., and line no.
15. Miscellaneous. (Valuable genealogical data is often recorded in this space or on the reverse side of the card.)

Bishops' Report of L.D.S. Church Members, December 28, 1852: The bishops' report of L.D.S. Church members is a register of names of heads of households residing in various wards as of December 28, 1852. The names are arranged alphabetically by first letter of the surname under the ward of residence. There is an index to the wards, and the register contains 104 pages. The following wards are included in the register:

1. Salt Lake City Wards, First through Nineteenth.
2. Mill Creek Ward.
3. South Cottonwood Ward.
4. Big Cottonwood Ward.
5. Little Cottonwood Ward.
6. Willow Creek Ward.
7. American Fork Ward.
8. Provo Wards, First through Fifth.
9. Springville Ward.
10. Nephi City Ward.
11. Lehi City Ward.
12. Palmyra Ward.
13. Pleasant Grove Ward.
14. Payson Ward.
15. Summit Creek Ward.
16. Mountainville Ward.
17. Coal Creek Ward.
18. Tooele City Ward.
19. North Kanyon [sic.] Ward.
20. Kays Ward.
21. North Cottonwood Ward.
22. Centreville Ward.
23. Ogden City Ward.
24. Box Elder Ward.
25. Parowan Ward.
26. Cedar City Ward.

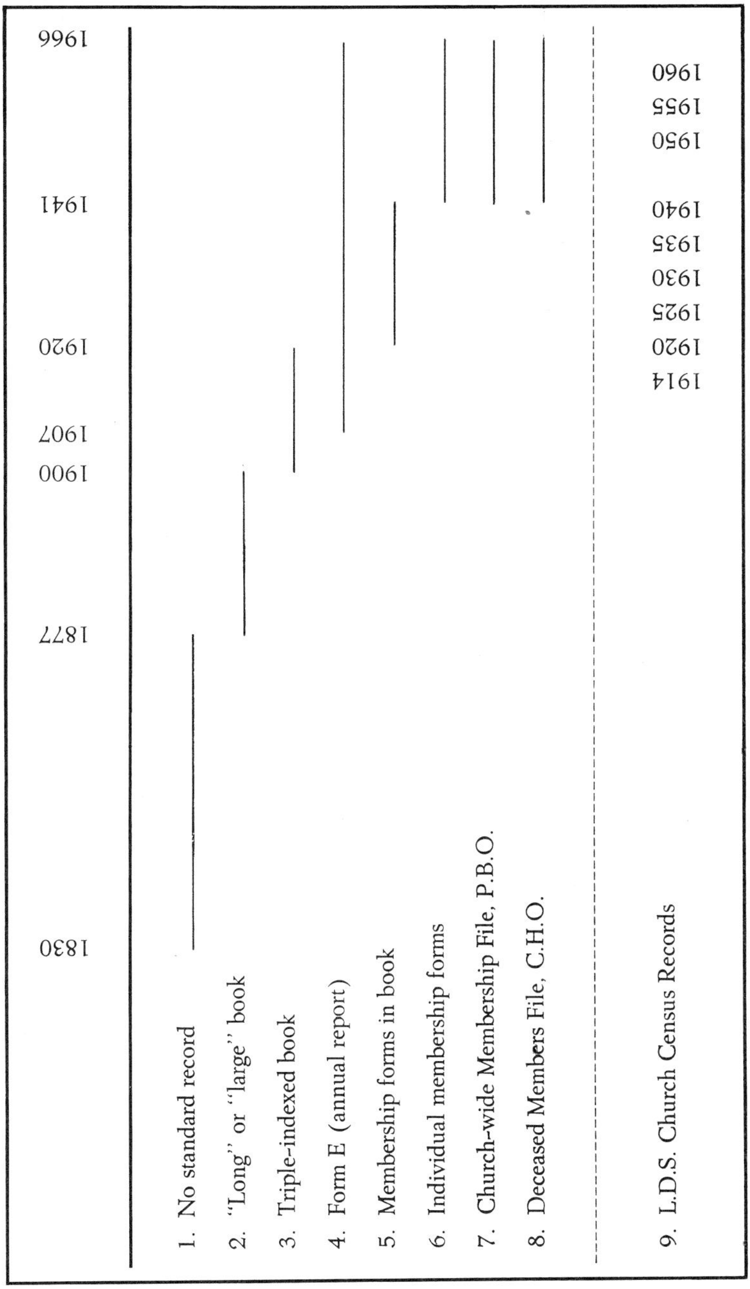

Figure 28. L.D.S. Church Membership Records.

1. No standard record
2. "Long" or "large" book
3. Triple-indexed book
4. Form E (annual report)
5. Membership forms in book
6. Individual membership forms
7. Church-wide Membership File, P.B.O.
8. Deceased Members File, C.H.O.

9. L.D.S. Church Census Records

1830 1877 1900 1907 1920 1941 1966

1914 1920 1925 1930 1935 1940 1950 1955 1960

AVAILABILITY

1. Ward (branch) membership record books, earliest to 1941 —microfilmed copy, library of The Genealogical Society; original, Church Historian's Office.

2. Form E (annual report) —microfilmed copy 1907 to 1947, and for some wards (branches) to 1951, library of The Genealogical Society; original, 1907-present, Church Historian's Office.

3. White records of living members—Ward (branch) clerk.

4. White records of deceased members (Deceased Members File) —Church Historian's Office.

5. Green records of living and deceased members—Presiding Bishop's Office.

6. Membership Card Index—microfilmed copy, library of The Genealogical Society; original, Church Historian's Office.

7. Bishops' Report of 1852—microfilmed copy, library of the Genealogical Society; original, Church Historian's Office.

GENEALOGICAL APPLICATION

1. Residence is established. The Membership Card Index, the Bishops' Report of 1852, the membership file in the Presiding Bishop's Office, and the Deceased Members File are aids in establishing wards in which individuals have resided. Other membership records may also give a ward (branch) of previous residence.

2. Membership records contain information about the first baptism and rebaptisms of members of The Church of Jesus Christ of Latter-day Saints. The earliest baptism date is the correct date to record on the family group record. Many proxy baptisms have been performed for persons who were baptized in life as a result of membership records not having been searched.

3. Many birth dates in membership records pre-date the commencement of vital registration in respective places of birth. (Before accepting the birth date, it should be determined who the informant

was and whether the birth date was recorded near the time of the event.)

4. The information may be from a primary source. The membership records often contain information a person gave about himself or immediate family.

5. Genealogical information regarding events in the lives of individuals was recorded in the Form E reports and other membership records concurrently.

6. Line of authority of ordination to the priesthood can be traced through membership records as the name of the individual who performed the ordination is recorded. One then finds the record of ordination of that individual, who often was a member of the same ward, and continues this procedure.

7. General information is given on names, places, dates, and relationships which may verify, or add to, presently known information and provides clues to records to be searched in both the survey phase and the research phase.

GENEALOGICAL LIMITATIONS

1. All of the ward records are not included in the Membership Card Index.

2. All of the information in the ward membership record books was not recorded at the time the event occurred, and may not be from a primary source.

3. Many ward records are incomplete, inaccurate, and sparsely documented.

4. Some of the records of members are missing.

5. An ordinance performed in other than a ward of residence is not recorded in the Form E of the home ward, but rather in the ward where the ordinance was performed.

6. If an event occurred in the stake jurisdiction, e.g., ordination to the offices of Elder, High Priest, etc., the stake clerk in recent

times has been responsible for forwarding this information to the ward clerk to be recorded on the individual's ward record of membership and in the appropriate place in the Form E. In earlier times, it was the ward clerk's responsibility to be aware of this type of event and obtain the information from the stake clerk. Consequently, the information was sometimes omitted from the Form E.

7. If information that should have been recorded in the Form E was omitted one year, it may be recorded in the Form E for the following year.

8. The Deceased Members File contains only records of members who have died since 1941 and whose deaths were reported to the Presiding Bishop's Office. (If a member has died since 1941, and his membership card is not in the Deceased Members File in the Church Historian's Office, it should be reported to the P.B.O. or C.H.O.)

PROJECT ASSIGNMENTS

1. Check your current record of membership.

2. Search the following sources if indicated on the family group record selected in Chapter 6:

a. Membership Card Index.

b. Bishops' Report of 1852.

c. Applicable ward (branch) membership records.

d. Form E reports to verify ordinance dates.

Chapter 17

L.D.S. CHURCH CENSUS RECORDS

TIME PERIOD

1914, 1920, 1925, 1930, 1935, 1940, 1950, 1955, and 1960.

ORIGIN

The Church of Jesus Christ of Latter-day Saints initiated census records to provide a church-wide file of information on L.D.S. families. (Prior to 1941 there was no church-wide file of membership records.) The Church census information for each family was recorded on a separate card by a census taker who was either a ward (branch) clerk or a member of the ward (branch), and who visited with each family to obtain the desired data. After the census information was gathered by the census taker and checked and verified with ward membership records by the ward (branch) clerk, the census cards from wards and branches of The Church were combined in Church-wide files. The 1914 through 1935 Church census cards were arranged together in one collection with all cards for a particular family filed together, the earliest census card first, and the groups of family cards arranged alphabetically by surname of the head of the household on the first card for each family, usually the father. If the father died during the years between the censuses, any census cards compiled after his death, which contained the names of the remaining members of the family were filed with previous cards for the particular family.

The census cards for the year 1940 were combined and arranged alphabetically by surname of the head of the household. The census cards for 1950 were originally combined and arranged alphabetically by surname of the head of the household and microfilmed. Recently the census cards for 1950, 1955, and 1960 have been combined with cards referring to a particular family filed together with earliest census first, and the groups of family cards arranged alphabetically by surname of the head of the household.

Included on the microfilmed copy of the 1914 through 1935 census, are some delayed birth certificates which originated in the Church Historian's Office. Delayed birth certificates are now kept in a separate file. (See Chapter 18.) Also on the microfilmed copy of the 1914 through 1935 census cards are a few genealogical survey cards which appear to contain information about individuals from Granite Stake (Salt Lake City, Utah).

CONTENTS

The L.D.S. Church census cards for the years 1914 through 1950 contain information as shown in the following example; the 1955 and 1960 census cards are similar to those of 1950.

Contents of L.D.S. Church Census Records

Information Requested	1914	1920	1925	1930	1935	1940	1950
Name of ward and stake	x	x	x	x	x	x	x
Date census was taken	x	x	x	x	x	x	x
By whom census was taken	x	x	x	x	x	x	x
Family name	x	x	x	x	x	x	x
Address	x	x	x	x	x	x	x
Name of father (husband, man)	x	x	x	x	x	x	x
Married name of mother (wife)	x						

Information Requested	1914	1920	1925	1930	1935	1940	1950
Maiden name of mother (wife, woman)		x	x	x	x	x	x
Names of children living at home	x	x	x	x	x	x	x
Sex	x	x	x	x	x	x	x
Age	x						
Date of birth		x	x	x	x	x	x
Place of birth (state or country)	x	x	x	x	x	x	x
Place of birth (town)					x	x	x
Priesthood, member, child, or non-member	x	x	x	x	x	x	x
Social relation (single, married, divorced, separated, widower, widow, unknown)	x	x	x	x	x	x	x
Ward membership record number	x	x	x	x	x		
If on record						x	x
Name of ward clerk	x	x	x	x	x	x	x
Ward and stake previously of record					x	x	x
Previous street address						x	x
Date moved to present address						x	x
Auxiliaries enrolled in		x					
Baptism and confirmation dates (missions only)				x			

The delayed birth certificates which originated in the Church Historian's Office and which were included in the 1914 through 1935 census cards, contain the following information: date certificate issued; name, date, and place of birth of individual; name of father; maiden name of mother; and date of baptism in the L.D.S. Church and by whom.

The genealogical survey cards included in the 1914 through 1935 census cards include the following information: name of individual; address; religious denomination; occupation; name of father; name of mother; name of spouse's father; name of spouse's mother; date christened or blessed and by whom; date confirmed and by whom; date ordained to the Priesthood, to what office, and by whom; date and place of marriage and to whom; date of temple ordinances (baptism, endowment, sealing to wife, and sealing to parents) and whether by self or proxy; date and place of death; date and place of burial; relationship of heir; and source of information.

AVAILABILITY

1. Microfilmed copy of L.D.S. Church census records, 1914, 1920, 1925, 1930, 1935, 1940, and 1950—library of the Genealogical Society.

2. Original, 1914, 1920, 1925, 1930, 1935, and 1940—destroyed; 1950, 1955, and 1960—Church Historian's Office.

GENEALOGICAL APPLICATION

1. The names of members of a family group are listed together.

2. The name of the ward (branch) is determined which is necessary for searching ward (branch) records. (See Chapter 16.)

3. Residence is established. The place of residence indicates the geographic locality for searching records in the research phase.

4. The date of the census establishes residence at a specific period of time.

5. Many birth dates pre-date the commencement of vital registration in respective places of birth.

6. An age (1914 census) at a dated event is an aid in calculating a birth year.

7. The information given may be from a primary source. The census records often contain information a person gave about himself or his family.

8. General information is given on names, places, dates, and relationships which may verify, or add to, presently known information and provides clues to records to be searched in both the survey phase and research phase.

GENEALOGICAL LIMITATIONS

1. The L.D.S. Church census records are incomplete. The census was initiated in the stakes a few years earlier than in the missions. Some wards and branches did not participate in the census.

2. The census cards are arranged alphabetically by head of the household only. Unless one knows the name of the head of the household, he may not find the desired information.

3. The information on indicated family groups may be inaccurate and/or incomplete. The only names listed are those of persons presently living in the home.

PROJECT ASSIGNMENT

1. Search all L.D.S. Church census records which may contain information concerning persons whose names appear on the family group record selected in Chapter 6.

Chapter 18

L.D.S. CHURCH HISTORICAL RECORDS

JOURNAL HISTORY OF THE CHURCH OF JESUS CHRIST OF LATTER-DAY SAINTS

Time Period: 1830-

Origin and Contents: The *Journal History of The Church of Jesus Christ of Latter-day Saints* (*Journal History*) is a collection of over 1,000 loose-leaf type books which have been compiled in manuscript form. The first part is retrospective and was compiled by Andrew Jenson, Assistant Church Historian; since his death, the *Journal History* has been kept current. It contains an account of certain L.D.S. Church members and important historical events regarding The Church of Jesus Christ of Latter-day Saints. Excerpts from private journals, clippings from newspapers, biographies, pioneer company rosters and histories, records of emigrating groups, various documents, etc., have been preserved in the *Journal History* where the information is arranged chronologically. *Supplements to the Journal History* contain information received too late for insertion chronologically in the *Journal History.*

A card index to the *Journal History* has been compiled; it is arranged alphabetically by subject and by surname of individuals. The information on the cards varies and usually the cards referring to individuals contain some information regarding the event with which the individual was associated.

The card index is divided into two parts, 1830-1900 and 1901-present, and is available to the public. (There is a Church Chronology File which is available to the public at the Church Historian's Office which contains information similar to that included in the card index to the *Journal History*, but the Church Chronology File is not as complete.)

Availability:

1. Index—Church Historian's Office.

2. Microfilmed copy of the *Journal History*, 1830-1870—Church Historian's Office.

3. Original Journal History, 1830-present—Church Historian's Office.

Genealogical Application:

1. The card index to the *Journal History* should be searched first and all information copied from the card(s).

2. The *Journal History* aids in establishing organization dates of stakes, wards, missions, conferences, and branches.

3. General information, and particularly biographical data, is given which may verify, or add to, presently known information and provides clues to further research.

Genealogical Limitations:

1. Some of the information is from a secondary source as the information was not recorded at the time the event occurred and/or was recorded by someone other than an eye-witness.

PRIESTHOOD QUORUM RECORDS

Origin and Contents: Priesthood Quorum records include minutes of quorum meetings, quorum membership rolls, historical accounts of social gatherings, ordinations to the priesthood, biographies of quorum members, histories of the organization of quorums, statistical reports, etc. Records of the High Priests, Elders, and Aaronic Priesthood (Priests, Teachers, and Deacons) do not contain as much genealogical information, nor are they as readily available as are the records of the Seventies.

The First Seven Presidents of the Seventy have jurisdiction over Seventies Quorum records, and many of the earlier records were deposited in the office of the Seventies in the Church Office Building and then transferred to the Church Historian's Office.

The Seventies Quorum records include records of the first seventy Elders ordained to the office of a Seventy in 1835 and 1836, and genealogical information on the members of quorums 1 to 90 in 1876, and the presidents of quorums 1 to 224, undated. There are indexes to many of the records of quorum members, including one to records of members of quorums 1 to 90 in 1876 which has been arranged in alphabetical order by surname. The Seventies office has compiled an alphabetical list of stakes indicating the number (name) of the Seventies Quorums and the wards assigned to that quorum.

The genealogical information in the Seventies Quorum records includes the following:

1. Number (name) of quorum.
2. Name of Seventy.
3. Date and place of birth.
4. Parentage (includes mother's maiden surname).
5. Date of baptism and by whom.
6. Date of ordination to the office of Seventy and by whom.
7. Residence.

Availability:

1. Microfilmed copies of Seventies Quorum records—library of The Genealogical Society.

2. Original Priesthood Quorum Records—Church Historian's Office.

Genealogical Application:

1. Indexes should be searched first.

2. The information may be from a primary source as the records often contain information a person gave about himself.

3. General information is given about names, places, dates, and relationships which may verify, or add to, presently known information and provides clues to further research.

Genealogical Limitation:

1. Many priesthood quorum records have not been indexed.

CARD INDEX TO PATRIARCHAL BLESSINGS

Time Period: 1833-

Origin and Contents: A Patriarchal Blessing is a blessing given to members of The Church of Jesus Christ of Latter-day Saints by a Patriarch. (Individuals may obtain copies of their own Patriarchal Blessing, a husband may obtain a copy of the blessing of his wife, and a wife that of her husband. Children must obtain written permission from their parents before obtaining a copy of the parents' blessing, and the same rule applies in obtaining a copy of the blessing of brothers and sisters. Blessings of deceased persons will not be copied. In order to read the Patriarchal Blessing of a more distant relative, one must obtain permission from the Church Historian.)

There is an alphabetical card index to Patriarchal Blessings; it lists names of persons who have received Patriarchal Blessings and for whom a copy of the blessing has been filed with the Church Historian's Office. It is not unusual to find more than one index card for an individual. The index card includes only the genealogical data given in the blessing and may include the following:

1. Name of individual.

2. When born.

3. Where born.
4. Name of father.
5. Name of mother.
6. Date of blessing.
7. Place of blessing (ward and stake or town and state).
8. Lineage.
9. Patriarch giving blessing.
10. Reference to volume and page no. in the Church Historian's Office.

Availability:

1. Microfilmed copy of index—library of The Genealogical Society.
2. Original index—Church Historian's Office.
3. Copies of Patriarchal Blessings—Church Historian's Office.

Genealogical Application:

1. The information may be from a primary source. The card index often contains information an individual gave about himself.
2. General information is given on names, places, dates, and relationships which may verify, or add to, presently known information and provides clues for further research.

Genealogical Limitation:

1. Only copies of blessings filed with the Church Historian's Office have been indexed. Some were never turned in.

MISSIONARY RECORDS

Time Period: 1830-

Origin and Contents: The missionary records are records of names of persons who have served full-time missions for The Church of Jesus Christ of Latter-day Saints; the records have been kept in chronological order. Records of missionaries prior to 1860 are retrospective, and a biographical sketch may be included. The missionary record books include names of missionaries, one per line, and include the following information:

1. Name of missionary.
2. Father's name.
3. Mother's maiden name.
4. Date of birth.
5. Place of birth.
6. Date of baptism and by whom.
7. Priesthood.
8. Quorum of membership.
9. Present residence.
10. Where sent.
11. When set apart and by whom.
12. Date sent.
13 Date returned.
14. Name of ward and stake.

There is an alphabetical card index to the missionary records.

Availability:

1. Microfilmed hand-written index 1860-1894—library of The Genealogical Society.

2. Original index 1830-present—Church Historian's Office.

3. Microfilmed copy of missionary records—library of The Genealogical Society.

4. Original missionary records—Church Historian's Office.

Genealogical Application:

1. To use original records without the index, one must know the date the missionary departed.

2. The information may be from a primary source. The records often contain information an individual gave about himself.

3. General information is given on names, places, dates, and relationships which may verify, or add to, presently known information and provides clues for further research.

Genealogical Limitation:

1. Information in missionary records prior to 1860 is retrospective and names of some missionaries may have been omitted from the records.

STAKE AND MISSION RECORDS

Origin and Contents: Historical Records of stakes and missions contain accounts of historical events, social gatherings, minutes of meetings, executive and council meetings, conferences, baptismals, ordinations to offices in the Melchizedek Priesthood, Priesthood Auxiliary events, statistical reports, etc. There are other types of historical records called manuscript histories which are compiled in the Church Historian's Office in manuscript form with excerpts from the Historical Records, journals, diaries, newspapers, publications, etc., pertaining to the particular jurisdiction. The Historical Records are not indexed; there are indexes to some of the manuscript histories (indexes of some missions are arranged by conference [district] and/or branch). Indexes to the manuscript histories include the following:

1. Argentine Mission.
2. Australian Mission.
3. British Mission.
4. California Mission.
5. Canadian Mission.
6. Central States Mission.
7. Czechoslovakian Mission.
8. Danish-Norwegian Mission.
9. East Central States Mission.
10. East German Mission.
11. Eastern States Mission.
12. East Indian Mission.
13. French Mission.
14. Franco-Belgian Mission.
15. French East Mission.
16. German Mission.
17. German-Austrian Mission.
18. Great Lakes Mission.
19. Hawaiian Mission.
20. Indian Territory Mission.
21. Italian Mission.
22. Las Vegas Mission.
23. Malta Mission.
24. Mexican Mission.
25. Middle States Mission.
26. Netherlands Mission.
27. North Central States Mission
28. North Argentine Mission
29. Northern States Mission.
30. Northwestern States Mission.

31. Norwegian Mission.
32. Samoan Mission.
33. San Bernardino Mission.
34. Scandinavian Mission.
35. Society Islands Mission.
36. South African Mission.
37. South American Mission.
38. Southern States Mission.
39. Southwestern States Mission.
40. Swedish Mission.
41. Swiss Mission.
42. Swiss-Italian Mission.
43. Swiss-German Mission.
44. Tongan Mission.
45. Turkish Mission.
46. Western States Mission.

Availability:

1. Card index to manuscript histories—room 305, Church Office Building.

2. Manuscript histories—Church Historian's Office.

3. Historical Records—Church Historian's Office.

Genealogical Application:

1. The card index refers to manuscript histories where additional information may be found, and where a date may indicate an entry in the Historical Records. (Baptism dates may be established. Many early L.D.S. Church members were baptized at conference [district] meetings.)

2. General information may be given on names, places, dates, and relationships which may verify, or add to, presently known information and provides clues to records to be searched in both the survey phase and the research phase.

Genealogical Limitations:

1. The card index to manuscript histories is incomplete.

2. The Historical Records are not indexed.

3. There is uncertainty as to the amount of genealogical information in the manuscript histories and Historical Records.

WARD AND BRANCH RECORDS

Origin and Contents: Historical Records are also kept in the wards and branches of The Church of Jesus Christ of Latter-day

Saints and include minutes of executive meetings, minutes of baptismals, minutes of Fast and Testimony meetings, minutes of Sacrament Meetings, records of persons set apart for Church positions, accounts of social events and gatherings, minutes of dedications, minutes of Priesthood Auxiliary meetings, various types of statistical reports, etc., compiled by clerks, secretaries, and historians. (These records may give the number of persons rather than names.)

Availability:
1. Historical Records—Church Historian's Office.

Genealogical Application:
1. General information may be given on names, places, dates, and relationships which may verify, or add to, presently known information and provides clues for records to be searched in both the survey and research phase.

Genealogical Limitations:
1. Historical Records are not indexed.
2. There is uncertainty as to the genealogical information contained in the Historical Records.

DEATH REGISTRATION

Time Period: 1848-

Origin and Contents: Registration of deaths, and some still-births, in Salt Lake City was initiated in the jurisdiction of the L.D.S. Church and later continued by civil authorities, 1890 in the Salt Lake City jurisdiction and 1905 in the state jurisdiction. The earliest registrations are one-line entries; the later ones are recorded in certificate form. Indexes have been compiled. The early death records in the L.D.S. Church jurisdiction may contain the following information:

1. Certificate or entry no.
2. Ward.
3. Name of deceased.
4. To whom related.

5. Son or daughter of.
6. Spouse of.
7. Birth date and place.
8. Death date, and cause.
9. Medical attendant.
10. Burial plot, block, and lot.

Later registration of deaths may contain additional information:

11. Occupation of deceased.
12. Address of deceased.
13. Citizenship.
14. Name and address of informant.
15. Mother's maiden name.
16. Name of cemetery.
17. Name and address of funeral director.
18. Whether the deceased was in the U.S. Armed Forces.
19. Whether single, married, widowed or divorced.

Availability:

1. Microfilmed copy of registered deaths, 1848-September 1950—library of The Genealogical Society.
2. Original—1848-1890, Church Historian's Office; 1890-1904, Salt Lake City Board of Health; 1905-present, Division of Vital Statistics, State Department of Health, Salt Lake City, Utah.

Genealogical Application:

1. The early records of deaths pre-date vital registration in the civil jurisdiction.
2. General information is given on names, places, dates, and relationships which may verify, or add to, presently known information and provides clues to records to be searched in both the survey phase and the research phase.

Genealogical Limitation:

1. The early registers of deaths in the L.D.S. Church jurisdiction include names of persons who died in Salt Lake City only.

DELAYED BIRTH CERTIFICATES

Origin and Contents: The Church Historian's Office issues delayed birth certificates for members of the L.D.S. Church when requested by the members. A copy is kept in the Church Historian's Office in an alphabetical file; women may be listed under either the maiden or married surname. The information for the certificates is obtained from L.D.S. Church records such as census and membership records. The delayed birth certificates may contain the following information:

1. Date of issue.
2. Name.
3. Date of birth.
4. Place of birth.
5. Name of father.
6. Maiden name of mother.
7. L.D.S. Church record source.
8. L.D.S. Church blessing and/or baptism date.

Availability:

1. Original delayed birth certificates—Church Historian's Office.

2. Some delayed birth certificates are on microfilm with L.D.S. Church census records, 1914-1935. (See Chapter 17.)

Genealogical Application:

1. Many of these certificates pre-date civil registration of vital statistics in the respective places of birth.

2. General information is given on names, places, dates, and relationships which may verify, or add to, presently known information and provides clues to records to be searched in both the survey phase and the research phase.

3. Information may be obtained for L.D.S. Church members regardless of geographical location of birth.

Genealogical Limitations:

1. The information may be from a secondary source, as the information was often recorded many years after the birth of the individual.

2. A delayed birth certificate is not filed for every member of the L.D.S. Church, but only for those who requested certificates.

MISCELLANEOUS

Additional L.D.S. Church historical records which may be of value to the genealogical researcher are biographies, autobiographies, journals, diaries, letters, documents, photographs, newspapers and periodicals, and L.D.S. school records. Many of these have been indexed and are available at the Church Historian's Office to those who identify themselves and state in detail the purpose of their research.

PROJECT ASSIGNMENT

1. Continue research on the family group record selected in Chapter 6 by searching the following where applicable:

a. Card indexes to *Journal History*, 1830-1900 and 1901-present, and *Journal History of the Church of Jesus Christ of Latter-day Saints.*

b. Priesthood Quorum records, particularly the Seventies.

c. Card index to Patriarchal Blessings.

d. Missionary Records and card index.

e. Stake and Mission Records, particularly the card index to manuscript histories.

f. Ward and Branch records.

g. L.D.S. Church death registers.

h. L.D.S. Church delayed birth certificates.

SUGGESTED READING

Office of the Church Historian, "Guide to the Historian's Office Library-Archives." Salt Lake City: The Church of Jesus Christ of Latter-day Saints, 1966.

Chapter 19

TEMPLE ORDINANCE RECORDS

There are various ordinances and ceremonies performed for both the living and the dead in the temples of The Church of Jesus Christ of Latter-day Saints. At certain times in the early history of The Church, when no temple was available, these ordinances were performed in places other than a temple and with the same authority as if they had been performed in the temple. All of these ordinances are referred to as "temple ordinances."

For genealogical purposes one is concerned with the ordinances listed on the family group record prepared by The Genealogical Society of The Church of Jesus Christ of Latter-day Saints, Inc.:

1. Baptisms.
2. Endowments.
3. Sealings of couples.
4. Sealings of children to parents.

When a genealogical researcher considers the term, "sealing," he determines if this is a sealing of couples (wife to husband) or a sealing of families (children to parents). Then he determines whether the sealing ceremony was for living individuals, deceased individuals, or living and deceased individuals. This information is necessary for obtaining the correct record book.

When an ordinance is performed on behalf of a deceased individual, the deceased person is represented by a living proxy, thus the term "proxy baptism," "proxy endowments," and "proxy sealings." This is the same as "baptisms for the dead," "endowments for the dead," and "sealings for the dead."

ORIGIN

Revelation concerning temple ordinances was given gradually, and practices accepted as proper today were not always observed in the early days of The Church. Frequently, sealings of living couples and sealings of a deceased to a living companion were performed in places other than a dedicated temple. Endowments for many persons were performed after the sealing of a couple; and, there were no sealings of children to parents (other than a very few in Nauvoo), and no endowments for the dead until 1877 in the St. George Temple.

Baptisms: The principle of baptism for the dead was first revealed to the general membership of The Church on August 15, 1840, and the first recorded baptisms for the dead were performed in the Mississippi River in September, 1840. It was later determined that these baptisms were not valid as witnesses and recorders were not present. On July 12, 1841, John Patton was appointed recorder of baptisms for the dead, and the members continued proxy baptisms in the Mississippi River. On October 3, 1841, it was revealed that baptisms for the dead should not be performed until the baptismal font in the Nauvoo Temple was completed. Baptisms for the dead were performed in the Nauvoo Temple from 1841 until 1846, however, the records are available only through January 9, 1845. From 1846 until the Endowment House was dedicated in 1855, there were no baptisms for the dead performed. The Endowment House proxy baptism records are available from 1857 through October 26,

1876. The next baptisms for the dead were performed in the St. George Temple in 1877 and since then, baptisms for the dead have been performed continuously in various temples.

One generally thinks of baptisms in the temple as being for the dead only; however, some baptisms for the living have been performed in temples when other baptismal fonts were not as readily available, or when many individuals were baptized on the same day. These baptisms were recorded by both ward clerks and temple recorders. There were also *re-baptisms* of living L.D.S. Church members, performed in the Logan Temple from 1884-1914. These re-baptisms are referred to as "renewal of covenants" and are recorded separately from first baptisms for the living which were performed in the Logan Temple.

Endowments: On May 4, 1842 a few endowments for the living were performed above Joseph Smith's store, and from January 11 to February 22, 1846 in the Nauvoo Temple. Endowments for the living were performed in places other than a temple after the Saints reached the Salt Lake Valley, the first available record beginning with February 20, 1851. The Endowment House was dedicated on May 5, 1855, and endowments for the living were performed there until 1884.

There were no endowments for the dead performed until the dedication of the St. George Temple in 1877, *resulting in a 37 year lapse between the first baptisms for the dead and the first endowments for the dead.*

Sealings of Couples: The first sealings of living couples were performed April 5, 1841 prior to the dedication of the Nauvoo Temple. Sealings of living couples and sealings of couples where one spouse was deceased were performed in the Nauvoo Temple from January 9 to February 22, 1846. Sealings of living couples and sealings of couples where one spouse was deceased were continued at Winter Quarters and in other places until the dedication of the Endowment House in 1855. Sealings of living couples continued to be performed in places other than a temple until the early 1900's. These were performed in homes, tithing offices, the President's Office, ward chapels, etc. After the dedication of the St. George Temple, these sealings were generally confined to the areas of Colorado, Old Mexico, and Arizona. These sealings are considered valid if there is a properly signed certificate, or if a record is found in a temple sealing book. Many of these sealings performed outside a temple are recorded in the Salt Lake Temple records; others are recorded in a record labeled Utah Sealings.

The practice of sealing living couples and couples where one spouse was deceased in places other than a temple has resulted in many couples being sealed prior to the endowment.

Sealings of Children to Parents: Sealings of children to parents were performed in the Nauvoo Temple from January 11 to February 6, 1846. These appear to be sealings of living children to living parents as no proxies are recorded. After the Saints left Nauvoo *there were no sealings of children (living or dead) to parents until the dedication of the St. George Temple in 1877, a time lapse of 31 years.* From 1877 to the present, sealings of children (living and/or dead) have been performed continuously.

CONTENTS

In each temple, recorders generally keep a separate record book for each ordinance, which could result in as many as nine different records being kept concurrently in each temple:

1. Baptisms for the living.
2. Re-baptisms for the living (Logan only).
3. Baptisms for the dead.
4. Endowments for the living.
5. Endowments for the dead.
6. Sealing of living couples.
7. Sealing of living to deceased spouse.
8. Sealing of deceased couples.
9. Sealing of children to parents.

Each record book includes the name of the temple, name of the ordinance, date of the ordinance, names of the officiators, names of the witnesses, and names of the recorders. The content and format

Figure 29. Chronology of Temple Ordinances.

Time Period or Temple Dedicated	Baptisms Living	Baptisms Dead	Endowments Living
Kirtland 27 Mar 1836	None	None	None
Pre-Nauvoo Period	None	Sep 1840– 3 Oct 1841	4 May 1842
Nauvoo Temple 1 May 1846	None	21 Nov 1841– 9 Jan 1845	10 Dec 1845– 7 Feb 1846
Pre-Endowment House Period	None	None	20 Feb 1851– 24 Apr 1854
Endowment House 5 May 1855	None	23 Oct 1857– 26 Oct 1876	5 May 1855– 6 Oct 1884
St. George 6 Apr 1877	5 Sep 1882–	9 Jan 1877	11 Jan 1877–
Logan 17 May 1884	21 May 1884–	21 May 1884–	21 May 1884–
Manti 21 May 1888	4 Sep 1888–	29 May 1888–	30 May 1888–
Salt Lake 6 Apr 1893	None	23 May 1893–	24 May 1893–
Hawaiian 27 Nov 1919	None	2 Dec 1919–	3 Dec 1919–
Alberta 26 Aug 1923	None	6 Nov 1923–	29 Aug 1923–
Arizona 23 Oct 1927	31 Mar 1928–	26 Oct 1927–	27 Oct 1927–
Idaho Falls 23 Sep 1945	None	3 Dec 1945–	5 Dec 1945–
Swiss 11 Sep 1955	None	1 Oct 1955–	16 Sep 1955–
Los Angeles 11 Mar 1956	None	24 Mar 1956–	16 Apr 1956–
New Zealand 20 Apr 1958	None	22 Apr 1958–	24 Apr 1958–
London 7 Nov 1958	None	10 Sep 1958–	10 Sep 1958–
Oakland 16 Nov 1964	None	1 Dec 1964–	5 Jan 1965–

Endowments Dead	Sealings Couples Living	Sealings Couples Liv/Dead	Sealings Couples Dead	Sealings Children Liv/Dead
None	None	None	None	None
None	5 Apr 1841	None	None	None
None	9 Jan 1846–22 Feb 1846	9 Jan 1846–22 Feb 1846	None	11 Jan 1846–6 Feb 1846
None	8 Nov 1846–5 May 1855	8 Nov 1846–5 May 1855	None	None
None	5 May 1855–22 Sep 1889	5 May 1855–22 Sep 1889	5 May 1855–22 Sep 1889	None
11 Jan 1877–	11 Jan 1877–	11 Jan 1877–	11 Jan 1877–	22 Mar 1877–
21 May 1884–	21 May 1884–	21 May 1884–	21 May 1884–	21 May 1884–
30 May 1888–	30 May 1888–	30 May 1888–	30 May 1888–	6 June 1888–
24 May 1893–	24 May 1893–	23 Apr 1893	23 Apr 1893–	8 Apr 1893–
3 Dec 1919–	3 Dec 1919–	3 Dec 1919–	3 Dec 1919–	3 Dec 1919–
29 Aug 1923–	29 Aug 1923–	7 Nov 1923–	7 Nov 1923–	29 Aug 1923–
27 Oct 1927–	27 Oct 1927–	27 Oct 1927–	27 Oct 1927–	27 Oct 1927–
5 Dec 1945–	5 Dec 1945–	5 Dec 1945–	5 Dec 1945–	5 Dec 1945–
16 Sep 1955–	16 Sep 1955–	16 Sep 1955–	16 Sep 1955–	16 Sep 1955–
14 Apr 1956–	30 Mar 1956–	30 Mar 1956–	30 Mar 1956–	16 Apr 1956–
24 Apr 1958–	24 Apr 1958–	24 Apr 1958–	24 Apr 1958–	24 Apr 1958–
10 Sep 1958–	10 Sep 1958–	10 Sep 1958–	10 Sep 1958–	10 Sep 1958–
19 Dec 1964–	21 Dec 1964–	5 Jan 1965–	14 Jan 1965–	5 Jan 1965–

of each record varies as does the genealogical information given. Surnames of women may be recorded as maiden and/or married.

Baptisms: Many of the baptisms for the dead performed in the Mississippi River and in the Nauvoo Temple were performed with male proxies for females, and female proxies for males; for this reason many of the proxy baptisms for this period are not valid. However, the records have been preserved and are valuable because of the genealogical information given. The content and format of the baptism records vary for each time period and each temple, but may include the following:

Living—
1. Name.
2. When born.
3. Where born.
4. Father's name.
5. Mother's name.
6. Date baptized.
7. By whom baptized.
8. Date confirmed.
9. By whom confirmed.

Deceased—
1. Name.
2. When born.
3. Where born.
4. When died.
5. Name of proxy.
6. Name of heir.
7. Relationship of heir to deceased.

Endowments: More information is generally recorded in endowment records than in the other temple ordinance records and may include the following:

1. Name.
2. When born.
3. Where born.
4. Father's name.
5. Mother's maiden name.
6. When married.
7. Name of spouse.

If deceased—
8. When died.
9. Name of heir.
10. Name of proxy.
11. Relationship of heir to deceased.

Sealing of Couples: Prior to the opening of the St. George Temple, sealings of living couples and sealings of a deceased to a living companion were recorded in the same record book. Records kept after the dedication of the St. George Temple generally contain the sealings of living couples in one record book and combine the sealings of a living to a deceased companion in the same record book with sealings of dead couples. Information in the sealing records varies but may include the following:

1. Name of husband.	If deceased—
2. Name of wife.	7. When husband died.
3. When husband born.	8. When wife died.
4. Where husband born.	9. Name of proxy.
5. When wife born.	10. Name of heir (relation-
6. Where wife born.	ship rarely given).

Sealing of Children to Parents: Records of sealings of children to parents include adoptions, and in early records all sealings of children to parents were termed "adoptions." Living and deceased individuals are recorded together in the same record book; information varies but may include the following:

1. Name of father.	10. Baptism dates (rarely).
2. Where father born.	11. Endowment dates (rarely)
3. When father born.	
4. Name of mother.	If deceased—
5. Where mother born.	12. Name of proxy.
6. When mother born.	13. Name of heir (relation-
7. Name of children.	ship rarely given).
8. Where children born.	14. Date of death of parents.
9. When children born.	15. Date of death of children.

INDEXES

Temple ordinance record books have been indexed and sometimes several are combined to form indexes for larger periods of time. Records of temple ordinances performed by living individuals for themselves are indexed by the name of the individual. Temple ordinances performed for deceased individuals are generally indexed under the name of the heir; the proxy was often the heir in early temple records. The term "instance of" is used in early records for the term "heir." Therefore, in order to use the index to proxy temple records, one must know the name of the heir or at whose "instance" the temple work was performed.

The heir was often the oldest male member of the family or the first individual to join The Church of Jesus Christ of Latter-day Saints, and his name was often used as heir long after his death. The term "family representative" is presently used in place of "heir," and the family representative must be a living individual, a blood relative to the deceased, and a baptized member of The Church of Jesus Christ of Latter-day Saints.

The Genealogical Society has prepared a card file (available on microfilm) listing the names of heirs in the Church up to 1941. In addition to the name of the heir, the card lists the names and addresses of those who submitted family group records to The Genealogical Society under the name of that particular heir. (These persons often hired research through the Research Department of The Genealogical Society. See Chapter 11.)

The method of indexing temple ordinance records varies with each temple, each time period, and each type of record.

Baptisms: There is no Church-wide index to temple baptisms; therefore, one must know the name of the temple where the baptism was performed.

Living—indexed by name of individual.

Dead—indexed by name of heir (Logan Temple 1884-1887 indexed by name of deceased).

There is a card index for baptisms for the dead for the pre-Nauvoo and Nauvoo Temple baptisms. The records are indexed by the name of the deceased individual and by the name of the proxy (heir). This card file is available at the library of The Genealogical Society.

Endowments: The Temple Records Index Bureau (see Chapter 12) is a Church-wide index to temple endowments, and one generally does not need to search the original record unless he suspects an error, or missing or misfiled card.

Living—indexed by name of individual.

Dead—indexed by name of heir (St. George Temple 1877-1910 indexed by name of deceased).

Sealing of Couples: There is no Church-wide index to sealings of couples, although the Nauvoo, pre-Endowment House, and some early Salt Lake Temple records have been indexed in the T.I.B. (orange cards). Sealing records for a deceased person sealed to a living companion may contain two indexes, one for the living individual, and one for the name of the heir.

Living—indexed by name of husband and by name of wife.

Dead—indexed by name of heir (St. George Temple 1877-1913 indexed by name of deceased).

Sealing of Children to Parents: There is no Church-wide index to sealings of children to parents although a few early Salt Lake Temple sealing records are indexed in the T.I.B. (orange cards). Names of living and deceased individuals are in the same record book; therefore, the indexes usually have two parts, one for living individuals and one for heirs. Children's names do not appear to be indexed.

Living—indexed by name of the father and the mother.

Dead—indexed by name of heir.

AVAILABILITY

1. Microfilmed temple records—library of The Genealogical Society. Call numbers to baptism records are available through the card catalogue; call numbers to endowment and sealing records are available through the Reference Department with special permission.

2. Original temple records—available at each temple and may be searched by those holding a temple recommend. Pre-Nauvoo, Nauvoo, pre-Endowment House, Endowment House, and sealings performed in other than a temple are all available in the Salt Lake Temple.

GENEALOGICAL APPLICATION

1. Temple ordinance records are used to verify temple ordinance dates. For endowment dates a search of the T.I.B. is considered adequate unless one suspects an error, or a missing or misfiled card.

2. Names of additional relatives may be found. An individual usually performed proxy ordinances for more than one relative on a given day. Records of these ordinances could reveal names of additional relatives, establish relationships, and provide the original, and therefore the correct, proxy ordinance date for relatives.

3. The information may be from a primary source. Temple ordinance records often contain information an individual gave about himself, or close relatives: brothers, sisters, aunts, uncles, cousins, parents, and grandparents.

4. General information is given on names, places, dates, and relationships which may verify, or add to, presently known information and provides clues to records to be searched in both the survey phase and the research phase.

GENEALOGICAL LIMITATIONS

1. Information is often inaccurate and incomplete.

2. The informant or source of information is often unidentifiable.

3. The stated relationships are often inaccurate, particularly for the terms "cousin" and "friend."

4. Some records are missing.

5. There is no Church-wide index to baptisms and sealings. Records for each ordinance and for each temple are indexed separately. One must determine the specific temple, time period, and condition (living or deceased) in order to use the indexes.

6. There is uncertainty as to which sealing records are indexed in the T.I.B.

7. Temple ordinances for the dead are usually indexed by the name of the heir rather than by the name of the individual.

PROJECT ASSIGNMENT

1. Search the original temple ordinance records as indicated on the family group record selected for research in Chapter 6.

SUGGESTED READING:

Lundwall, N. B. *Temples of the Most High.* Salt Lake City: Bookcraft, 1952.

Talmage, James E. *The House of the Lord.* 3d. ed.; Salt Lake City: Bookcraft, 1962.

Chapter 20

ASSISTANCE WITH THE SURVEY

If at all possible, each individual should complete his own research survey. The search in the home jurisdiction can be successfully accomplished through personal interviews and correspondence; printed family histories, maps, and gazetteers can be used at a local library. However, the search in L.D.S. Church records requires that one use the facilities of the library of The Genealogical Society or one of its branches. Often this is impossible, and the next best step is to cooperate with a relative or a family organization to search the necessary records.

THE GENEALOGICAL RESEARCH SPECIALIST

If it is impossible to search the records through a relative or a family organization, one should consider engaging a genealogical research specialist. The competent genealogical researcher must understand the history, geography, and social customs of the locality in question. Having been born and raised in a specific locality or country, or familiarity with the language, does not make one a genealogical research specialist for the geographic area. A research specialist must be able to define and detail research objectives; have an understanding of the origin, content, availability, genealogical application, and genealogical limitations of each record; and possess the ability to analyze these records in the light of genealogical evidence. He recognizes the difference between quality and quantity in genealogical research and has a working knowledge of certain methods, tools, procedures, and techniques associated with his area of specialization. Finally, he is able to compile complete and accurate pedigrees and family group records. These qualifications enable him to make the best possible use of his time and his client's funds.

THE CLIENT

The client (sometimes referred to as the patron) who engages the research specialist may be one individual or a group of individuals, such as a family organization. Since the cost of research can be expensive over a period of time, it is to the advantage of the individual to join or to form a family organization, (see Chapter 7), wherein many persons contribute toward the research.

The more the client knows about genealogical research, the more satisfactory his relationship will be with a research specialist. The more competent research specialists would prefer working *with* an individual, rather than *for* an individual. A client who has a knowledge of correct procedures and record sources can better evaluate the work of the research specialist.

A genealogical research specialist should be willing to work with family members to teach them correct research procedures, or to suggest ways in which the family can assist the research specialist, thus saving time and expense and allowing the client to perform his own research whenever possible.

Meetings could be scheduled where the researcher meets with family members and explains the research problems and assignments. The researcher and the family members should study the records together to be certain proper instructions are given and being followed. It is wise for the family members to make carbon copies of their work, one for themselves, one for the researcher, and one for the family genealogical chairman.

Branch libraries of The Genealogical Society make it possible for family members in different parts of the United States to participate. One family organization purchases microfilms to be read by the family genealogical chairman, who lives in Oklahoma. Other family members in the Utah area meet with the family's research specialist at the branch library of The Genealogical Society in Provo, Utah for consultation. Many of these family members return to Salt Lake City and do the assigned research at the library of The Genealogical Society. Still other family members, who live near branch libraries in Arizona and California, are given instructions by mail and assigned carefully selected films.

The family genealogical chairman and the genealogical research specialist receive copies of searches made by family members, and they carefully analyze and discuss together the pedigree problems. If the family genealogical chairman is not skilled in analyzing, the research specialist should do this portion of the survey. By using this type of arrangement, family members can search all records of the survey phase.

The client should have an understanding with the researcher as to what research is expected and which lines of the pedigree to follow. He supplies the researcher with *all known* information in his possession regarding his particular ancestral problem. All known information includes family group records, pedigree charts, traditions, previous research notes, etc. All too often, research is duplicated because information was withheld by the client. If at all possible, a visit between the client and the research specialist is desirable. The research specialist has a better opportunity to question the client as to exactly what has been done previously and what is expected of him.

Before any research is begun, there should be an understanding concerning the researcher's fees. The client is almost certain to get better quality research and true value for his money if he pays the researcher in advance. An advanced fee is protection for both the client and the researcher. This ensures the researcher's wage and indicates to him the amount of time the client wishes spent on the problem. Any time spent beyond the amount of deposit is at the researcher's own risk. It is suggested that the initial fee not exceed $20.00 after which a report should be written to the client so that he and the researcher can evaluate the work and make any decisions concerning further research. The client should beware of those who charge a specific fee for each name supplied, rather than charging an hourly fee. Paying by the name is not a measure of quality; it encourages gathering all names of a particular surname whether related to the individual or not.

The client should be aware that a research specialist cannot always produce positive results. He sells his services and searches the records. Research may be particularly difficult where many records have been damaged, destroyed, or lost; in some populous cities searches may be very extensive and time consuming; a difficult problem could be encountered if an ancestor moved frequently and the exact time he and his family resided in different localities cannot be determined.

The client is entitled to, and should receive, a report of the records searched. It is important to know which records were searched and what information was or was not found so that the search will not be repeated. The researcher could supply this information by giving the client a copy of the calendars of search along with a carbon copy of his research notes. In addition, there should be a written analysis of the work done to date, a suggestion of records to be searched, and an estimate of the number of hours required for future searches. If the client knows some of the procedures and methods of research, the report will be one way of evaluating the competency of the genealogical researcher.

COMMERCIAL FIRMS

One should beware of advertisements where commercial firms offer pedigrees for a specific price that may range from a few to hundreds of dollars. In exchange for his money the client is supplied with a printed pedigree with many names. There is no guarantee that any of the persons on the pedigree is of the client's ancestry, or that the work itself is a true pedigree.

Hand in hand with the selling of pedigrees is that of selling copies of family coats of arms. One must prove his descent from the person who originally received the coat of armour and prove legal heirship to be entitled to use a coat of arms.

Some commercial firms do not allow their clients to have personal contact with their researcher and refuse the client permission to examine the research notes. Much is lost to both the researcher and the client, and the only gain is with the commercial firm which collects a fee from the client above that which is paid the researcher. In distinguishing ". . . between the professional genealogist and the commercial houses, the difference of attitude is the essential thing. The commercial house does not feel the same sense of personal responsibility to the client: the emphasis is on giving the client what he wants, rather than on giving him the truth."[1]

THE AGENT

It becomes necessary for a genealogical research specialist to employ an agent to search books and records when they are not immediately available to him. The agent differs from the genealogical research specialist in that he does not attempt to analyze the research problem, but follows specific instructions under the direction of the research specialist. The agent makes the search, copies the information requested, and forwards it to the specialist. If no restrictions are put on the search, the agent might repeat previous searches for which the research specialist would not want to pay. The wise research specialist knows in advance the approximate cost of a search so that he is not confronted later with an exorbitant fee.

The agent's fee many vary according to the research request, from an hourly fee to a standard charge for a specific search. In addition to the search there may be a charge for travel expense.

A research specialist could serve as an agent for other research specialists or for individuals learning to perform their own research;

---

[1]Donald Lines Jacobus, *Genealogy as a Pastime and Profession* (New Haven, Conn.: The Tuttle, Morehouse, and Taylor Co., 1930), p. 54.

in which case he would extract the information requested but make no analysis of the problem.

CORRESPONDENCE

If a record is not located at the library of The Genealogical Society or in some other library, it does not mean that the record is not a valuable genealogical source. A resident of Salt Lake City conducting research in certain records in England could find that 90% of the research would necessitate use of local record repositories in England and would require much research by correspondence.

Many persons have expended large sums of money to hire individuals to travel throughout the United States and in foreign countries, or have traveled there themselves, for the purpose of searching records, when the records could have been searched by corresponding with an experienced agent, native to the area, for only a fraction of the cost.

One must frequently determine what record source to search, where it is available, and whether it is best to search this record in person or to hire an agent through correspondence.

The correct decision is determined by ones familiarity with the records available in the locality of search and also his familiarity with records which are available locally. These decisions must be made in relation to where the researcher is now residing.

A researcher living in Provo, Utah would probably search the Patriarchal Blessing Index at the branch library of The Genealogical Society rather than at the library of The Genealogical Society or the Church Historian's Office in Salt Lake City. A researcher residing in Oregon might request through correspondence that a relative in Salt Lake City make a search of the Patriarchal Blessing Index at the library of The Genealogical Society.

A genealogical researcher must learn which records are available, where these records can be searched, and decide the best means for searching them, either in person or by correspondence. Whether the researcher lives in Salt Lake City, Utah or London, England he cannot avoid research by correspondence.

The following letter may be useful for requesting a search in the Temple Records Index Bureau:

> Your address
>
> Temple Records Index Bureau
> The Genealogical Society
> 107 South Main Street
> Salt Lake City 11, Utah
>
> Gentlemen:
>
> Please search the Temple Records Index Bureau for all names underlined in red on the enclosed family group record(s) and make xerox copies of any cards found.
>
> Sincerely,
> Your name

If there is a copy of the family group record(s) in the Main Records Section of the Church Records Archives (indicated by a "P" and/or "C"), xerox copies of the Temple Records Index Bureau cards will not be made, and the patron should write to the Public Service Department and request a xerox copy of the family group record(s). A letter similar to the following is suggested:

> Your address
>
> The Public Service Department
> Library of The Genealogical Society
> 107 South Main Street
> Salt Lake City 11, Utah
>
> Gentlemen:
>
> Please search the Main Records Section (pink and white labeled binders) of the Church Records Archives for the following family group record(s) and make xerox copies of any family group records found:
>
> 1. Complete name of husband, birth date, birth place, and maiden name of wife.
> 2. Complete name of husband, birth date, birth place, and maiden name of wife.
> 3. etc.
>
> Sincerely
> Your name

It is suggested that no money be enclosed in the letters to The Genealogical Society as a statement will be sent to the patron if there is a charge. At the present time there is no charge for the T.I.B. search nor for the service in the Main Records Section of the Church Records Archives. The latter does not include a search in the Patron's Section (yellow labeled binders), nor in the Sealing Section (orange labeled binders).

To obtain additional information from the T.I.B. and from the few sources not available through branch libraries (records that are not microfilmed) it is suggested that one employ the services of an accredited researcher. When writing to an accredited researcher one should enclose all known information in the form of family group records and pedigree charts and be specific in his requests. The following letter may be useful as a guide:

Your address

Name and address of an accredited researcher

Dear

Enclosed are two family group records with corresponding pedigree chart. Xerox copies of Temple Records Index Bureau cards and copies of the family group records as found in the Main Records Section of the Church Records Archives are also enclosed.

Please search the Temple Records Index Bureau for additional temple work performed by these individuals or relatives, and continue the survey in L.D.S. Church records by searching the following sources for the individuals named on the family group records and pedigree chart:

(1) Surname Card Index.

(2) Early Church Information Card Index.

(3) Marriage License Card Index.

(4) File to Card-indexed Pedigree Charts.

(5) Patron's Section Family Group Records, 1962-present (yellow labels).

(6) Sealing Section Family Group Records, 1956-present (orange labels).

(Note: Letter continued on page 200.)

> Please send complete copies of all information found as I will continue the survey through film rental at the branch library.
>
> Enclosed is a check for $10.00 as a deposit for this work.
>
> Sincerely
Your name

SUGGESTED READING

Cache Genealogical Library. *Handbook for Genealogical Correspondence*. Salt Lake City, Utah: Bookcraft, 1963.

SECTION IV

DICTIONARY OF TERMS AND ABBREVIATIONS

ANNOTATED BIBLIOGRAPHY

DICTIONARY OF TERMS
AND ABBREVIATIONS

ABSTRACT, a summary of the important parts of a book, manuscript, document, etc.

ACCREDITED RESEARCHER, one who has passed a written and oral examination in genealogical research given by The Genealogical Society.

AGENT, one who is engaged to search specific records under the direction of a genealogical researcher; does not attempt to analyze the research problem.

ALIAS, an assumed name.

ANCESTOR, any person from whom one is descended in direct line.

ANNUAL REPORT, L.D.S. CHURCH, see Form E.

ARCHIVES, a place where public records, documents, etc., are kept; the public records, documents, etc., kept in such a place.

ARCHIVES OF THE GENEALOGICAL SOCIETY, see Church Records Archives.

ASCENDANT, an ancestor, or one who precedes in genealogical succession.

AUTOBIOGRAPHY, an account of a person's life written by himself.

BAPTISM, L.D.S. CHURCH, an ordinance performed in The Church of Jesus Christ of Latter-day Saints by those in authority, and received by persons who have reached the age of accountability, or 8 years of age; may be received by proxy for deceased individuals.

BIBLIOGRAPHY, a list of sources of information related to a given subject or author; also a list of literary works of a given author or publisher.

BIOGRAPHY, an account of one person's life written by another.

BOOK OF REMEMBRANCE, see Family Record Book.

BRANCH, L.D.S. CHURCH, see independent branch; see dependent branch.

C.H.O., see Church Historian's Office.

C.R.A., see Church Record Archives.

CALENDAR OF CORRESPONDENCE, a list of addresses where letters have been sent, indicating information desired, date sent, date reply received, and extract number in the research folder; serves as an index to correspondence.

CALENDAR OF SEARCH, a list, grouping, or systematic arrangement of items to be searched, items that have been searched, and where they can be located in the research folder and notebook; serves as an index to the items searched.

CALL NUMBER, the number assigned a book in a library; consists of a subject or classification number and an author, or Cutter number.

CATEGORY, see record category.

CEMETERY RECORD CATEGORY, an arbitrary grouping of records; includes cemetery records initiated by all 4 jurisdictions; see jurisdiction; see record category.

CENSUS, an official enumeration of persons.

CENSUS RECORD CATEGORY, an arbitrary grouping of records; includes census records initiated in the civil jurisdiction; see record category.

CENSUS RECORDS, L.D.S. CHURCH, 1914, 1920, 1925, 1930, 1935, 1940, 1950, 1955, and 1960; cards containing information about L.D.S. families.

CERTIFIED COPY, a copy of a record that has been attested to, or vouched for, as being an accurate copy and which bears a seal or signature, or both, of one in authority.

CHURCH HISTORIAN'S OFFICE (C.H.O.), a repository of records of the L.D.S. Church; address: Office of the Church Historian, Room 301, 47 East South Temple, Salt Lake City, Utah 84111.

CHURCH OFFICE BUILDING, address: Office of The Church of Jesus Christ of Latter-day Saints, 47 East South Temple, Salt Lake City, Utah 84111.

CHURCH RECORDS ARCHIVES (C.R.A.), a term which refers to pedigree charts and family group records filed in the library of The Genealogical Society.

CIRCUMSTANTIAL EVIDENCE, information which does not give a direct answer to a question, but with some inferences and calculations, implies a certain answer, or gives clues, which might lead to more direct evidence; see evidence.

CIVIL JURISDICTION, a sphere of authority; includes records originating as a result of government authority; see jurisdiction.

CLASSIFICATION NUMBER, part of a library book call number; denotes the subject of the book.

CLIENT, patron; in genealogical research, one who engages a genealogical researcher or genealogical research specialist.

COLLATERAL RELATIONSHIP, see relationship.

CONFERENCE, L.D.S. CHURCH, a geographic division within a mission; divided into branches; presently known as a district.

COPIED RECORD, copy of an original record; not a photostat.

COURT RECORD CATEGORY, an arbitrary grouping of records; includes court records initiated in civil and ecclesiastical jurisdictions; see record category.

CUTTER NUMBER, part of a library book call number; denotes the author of a book.

DECEASED MEMBERS FILE, L.D.S. CHURCH, a church-wide file containing records of deceased members who have died since 1941; located in the Church Historian's Office.

DELAYED BIRTH CERTIFICATE, a birth certificate compiled and issued many years after the birth occurred from information obtained from various sources.

DEPENDENT BRANCH, L.D.S. CHURCH, a geographic division within a mission; may be dependent upon, and in part, supervised by the nearest ward or branch.

DESCENDANT, one person who is descended from another.

DIRECT EVIDENCE, information which answers a question directly or which aids in a conclusion concerning a disputed issue; see evidence.

DISCREPANCY, conflicting evidence as a result of having obtained information from two or more sources.

DISTRICT, L.D.S. CHURCH, a geographic division within a mission; divided into branches; formerly known as a conference.

DOCUMENT, an original or official paper relied upon to record or prove something; to reference from sources as proof or support of information.

DOCUMENTARY TESTIMONY, testimony which has been written or recorded; may be either original or copied; see testimony.

e.g., for example.

EARLY CHURCH INFORMATION CARD INDEX, sometimes referred to as the Early Church Information File; an index of names of persons compiled from various L.D.S. Church and early Utah records; located at the library of The Genealogical Society.

ECCLESIASTICAL JURISDICTION, a sphere of authority; includes records kept by any and all religious denominations; see jurisdiction.

ECCLESIASTICAL RECORD CATEGORY, an arbitrary grouping of records; includes records initiated by the ecclesiastical jurisdiction, i.e., records initiated by any and all religious denominations; see record category.

ELEMENTS OF GENEALOGICAL IDENTITY, names, places, dates, and relationships.

EMIGRANT, one who emigrates; a person who departs from one region or country to settle in another.

EMIGRATE, to depart from one country or region to settle in another.

EMIGRATION-IMMIGRATION RECORD CATEGORY, an arbitrary grouping of records; includes records initiated in the civil jurisdiction and the social and commercial jurisdiction; see record category.

EMIGRATION REGISTERS OF CONTINENTAL EUROPE, registers compiled in L.D.S. Missions containing names of persons for whom arrangements were made for emigrating from the various countries to the United States (usually via Liverpool, England); have been referred to as Shipping Records, Emigration by Ship; Passenger Lists; and Emigration Records.

EMIGRATION REGISTERS OF THE BRITISH MISSION (1849-1885; 1899; 1925), registers compiled in the L.D.S. Church Liverpool, England Emigration Office listing names of L.D.S. Church sponsored emigrants from the British Isles and Continental Europe; have been referred to as Shipping Records, Emigrations by Ship; Passenger Lists; Emigration Records of the British Mission; and Liverpool Office Emigration Records.

ENDOWMENT, L.D.S. CHURCH, a series of ordinances performed in The Church of Jesus Christ of Latter-day Saints in the House of the Lord (Temples) by those in authority, and received by members of The Church in good standing; may be received by proxy for deceased individuals.

EUROPEAN EMIGRATION CARD INDEX (1849-1925), an index of names of persons who emigrated from European countries with L.D.S. Church sponsored groups of people; has been referred to as Crossing the Ocean, Emigration Card Catalogue, Shipping File Index, and Index to Shipping.

EVIDENCE, information resulting from testimony; proof for the establishing or disproving of an alleged fact. Evidence can be true or false, direct or circumstantial.

EXTRACT, excerpt; an exact copy of a portion of a book, manuscript, document, etc.

FAMILY GROUP RECORD, a graphic form on which identification (names, places, dates, and relationships) of an individual and/or family may be recorded.

FAMILY ORGANIZATION FILE, a card file which lists the names of family organizations; located at the library of The Genealogical Society.

FAMILY RECORD BOOK, a genealogical research tool; organized book, or compilation containing pedigree charts and family group records; sometimes referred to as "Book of Remembrance."

FAMILY REPRESENTATIVE, L.D.S. CHURCH, one who is responsible for the family genealogical research and temple work.

FINISHED SECTION, family group records (pink labels) for which all ordinance dates are completed; a part of the Main Records Section of the Church Records Archives.

FORM E, an annual report initiated in 1907 by The Church of Jesus Christ of Latter-day Saints; has been referred to as Transcript of Record of Members; includes information about missionaries, marriages, births and blessings, baptisms and confirmations, priesthood ordinations, deaths, divorces, and excommunications.

GENEALOGICAL RESEARCH, scientific genealogical research is systematic investigation of records to determine correct names, places, dates, and relationships pertaining to each individual ancestor and all members of his family.

GENEALOGICAL RESEARCH METHOD, (1) select an objective; (2) search the records; (3) evaluate the evidence.

GENEALOGICAL RESEARCH SPECIALIST, one who is skilled and experienced in genealogical research.

GENEALOGICAL SOCIETY, THE, address: The Genealogical Society of The Church of Jesus Christ of Latter-day Saints, Inc., 107 South Main Street, Salt Lake City, Utah 84111.

GENEALOGY, the study of individual or family descent with particular emphasis on names, places, dates, and relationships.

GENERATION, the average lifetime of a person; a single stage in the succession of natural descent—a parent, child, and grandchild represent three generations.

HEARSAY EVIDENCE, second-hand testimony.

HEIR, often the oldest male member of the family or the first individual to join The Church of Jesus Christ of Latter-day Saints and at whose instance temple ordinances have been performed.

HISTORICAL RECORDS, L.D.S. CHURCH, kept in stakes and missions, and wards and branches; contain accounts of historical events, social gatherings, minutes of meetings, executive and council meetings, conferences, baptismals, ordinations to office in the Priesthood, Priesthood auxiliary events, statistical reports, etc.

HOME JURISDICTION, a sphere of authority; all records which originate in the home are included in the home jurisdiction; see jurisdiction.

HOME RECORD CATEGORY, an arbitrary grouping of records; contains information from the home jurisdiction only; see record category.

i.e., that is.

ibid., in the same place; used to show further reference to a source cited just before.

IMMIGRANT, one who immigrates; one who enters and settles in a country or region foreign to him.

IMMIGRATE, to enter and settle in a foreign country or region.

IMMIGRATION, see emigration-immigration.

INDEPENDENT BRANCH, L.D.S. CHURCH, a geographic division within a mission or a stake; sometimes referred to as a branch.

J.H., see *Journal History of The Church of Jesus Christ of Latter-day Saints.*

JOURNAL HISTORY, see *Journal History of The Church of Jesus Christ of Latter-day Saints.*

JOURNAL HISTORY OF THE CHURCH OF JESUS CHRIST OF LATTER-DAY SAINTS (JOURNAL HISTORY), a collection of over 1,000 loose-leaf type books which have been compiled in manuscript form and which contain an account of events in the lives of certain L.D.S. Church members and important historical events regarding The Church of Jesus Christ of Latter-day Saints.

JURISDICTION, a sphere of authority; the authority or governing body which initiates the keeping of certain records. In genealogical research there are 4 jurisdictions: (1) home jurisdiction, (2) ecclesiastical (church) jurisdiction, (3) civil (government) jurisdiction, and (4) social and commercial jurisdiction.

L.D.S. CHURCH, see The Church of Jesus Christ of Latter-day Saints.

LAND RECORD CATEGORY, an arbitrary grouping of records; includes records concerning land transactions most often originating in the civil jurisdiction; see record category.

LIBRARY STACKS, library shelves.

LINEAGE, line of direct descent from an ancestor.

LINEAL RELATIONSHIP, see relationship.

MAIN RECORDS SECTION, a division of the Church Records Archives containing finished and unfinished sections.

MANUSCRIPT HISTORIES, L.D.S. CHURCH, histories compiled in the Church Historian's Office in manuscript form from the L.D.S. Church Historical Records, journals, diaries, newspapers, publications, etc.; e.g., Manuscript History of the British Mission.

MARRIAGE LICENSE CARD INDEX, sometimes referred to as the Miscellaneous Marriage Index; an index of names of persons compiled from marriage license records in some county courthouses in Utah, Idaho, and Wyoming; located at the library of The Genealogical Society.

MEMBERSHIP FILE, L.D.S. CHURCH, church-wide file of records of members; initated in 1941; in the Presiding Bishop's Office.

MIGRATE, to move from one place to another, usually from one part of a country to another.

MILITARY RECORD CATEGORY, an arbitrary grouping of records; includes military records initiated in the civil jurisdiction; see record category.

MISSION, L.D.S. CHURCH, a geographic division within the L.D.S. Church; corresponds in part with stake organizations; however, membership is usually relatively small and widely scattered; divided into districts (conferences) and branches.

MISSIONARY RECORDS, L.D.S. CHURCH, AND INDEX (1830-   ), genealogical data on missionaries.

Ms or Mss, manuscript, manuscripts.

n.d., no date.

n.p., no paging; no publisher.

NEE, born; used to introduce the maiden surname of a married woman.

OBITUARY CARD INDEX, sometimes referred to as Obituary File or Obituary Index; an index of names of persons whose obituaries have appeared in Salt Lake City newspapers and other miscellaneous records; located at the Church Historian's Office.

Op. cit., in the work cited.

ORAL TESTIMONY, statement or declaration spoken by word of mouth to establish proof or fact; see testimony.

ORDINANCES, L.D.S. CHURCH, see temple ordinances.

ORIGINAL RECORD, the first recording of an event in a particular record according to law or custom.

OUTFITTING STATION, a temporary L.D.S. Church settlement where L.D.S. pioneers obtained covered wagons, handcarts, and other supplies for their journey to Great Salt Lake Valley.

P.B.O. see Presiding Bishop's Office.

P. E. FUND CO., see Perpetual Emigrating Fund Company.

P.R.S. see Pedigree Referral Service.

PATRIARCHAL BLESSING, a blessing given to members of The Church of Jesus Christ of Latter-day Saints by a Patriarch.

PATRIARCHAL BLESSING CARD INDEX (1833-   ), a card index to Patriarchal Blessings filed in the Church Historian's Office.

PATRON, see client.

PATRONS SECTION, family group records submitted to The Genealogical Society for filing only; a part of the Church Records Archives.

PATRONYMIC, a surname derived from the name of a father or ancestor, e.g., John, son of Arvid, would be John Arvidson.

PEDIGREE, a recorded or known line of descent; a record of ancestry.

PEDIGREE CHART, a graphic form on which ancestry may be recorded.

PEDIGREE REFERRAL SERVICE (P.R.S.), a service of The Genealogical Society designed to help individuals and family organizations with their genealogical research by bringing together persons who have common lines of ancestry so they can coordinate and combine their research efforts and prevent duplication of research.

PERPETUAL EMIGRATING FUND COMPANY (P.E. FUND CO.), an L.D.S. organized loan company where emigrants could borrow money to finance their journey to Great Salt Lake Valley.

PHONETIC SPELLING, spelling of a word the way it sounds.

pp., pages.

PRESIDING BISHOP'S OFFICE (P.B.O.), address: Office of the Presiding Bishop, The Church of Jesus Christ of Latter-day Saints, 47 East South Temple, Salt Lake City, Utah 84111.

PRIMARY SOURCE OF TESTIMONY, testimony of an event by a participant or an eye-witness of the event at or near the time of the event; see testimony.

PRINTED SECONDARY RECORD CATEGORY, an arbitrary grouping of records, includes compilations made from other records; initiated in all jurisdictions; see record category; see jurisdiction.

PROGENITOR, an ancestor on the direct line.

PROOF, the establishment of fact by evidence; a preponderance of evidence.

PROXY, the authority to act for another; in the L.D.S. Church ordinances by proxy are performed for, and in behalf of, deceased individuals, males for males, females for females.

RECORD CATEGORY, an arbitrary grouping of similar or like records for convenience in studying and searching the records; in genealogical research there are 13: (1) home record category, (2) printed secondary record category, (3) vital (civil) record category, (4) cemetery record category, (5) census record category, (6) ecclesiastical (church) record category, (7) land record category, (8) probate record category, (9) court record category, (10) military record category, (11) emigration-immigration record category, and (12) social and commercial record category.

RECORDS OF MEMBERSHIP, L.D.S. CHURCH, records in book form and individual records of membership containing genealogical data on persons of the L.D.S. Church.

RELATIONSHIPS, of concern in genealogy: (1) lineal—between individuals in a direct line of descent from a common ancestor, (2) brother-sister—between individuals descended from the same parents, and (3) collateral—between two individuals having a common ancestor, but the lineal descent from that common ancestor is different.

RESEARCH FOLDER, a folder which contains research material: a status family group record, a pedigree chart, calendar of search, extracts from the research notebook, calendar of correspondence, copies of letters sent, replies received, and documents pertinent to the research problem.

RESEARCH NOTEBOOK, a collection of research notes in manuscript form; may be loose sheets of paper, spiral or ring binder, etc.

rev., revised.

SEALING, L.D.S. CHURCH, an ordinance performed in The Church of Jesus Christ of Latter-day Saints in the House of the Lord (Temples) by those in authority, and received by members of the Church in good standing; may be received by proxy for deceased individuals; there are sealings of couples (wife to husband) and sealings of families (children to parents).

SEALING SECTION, family group records submitted to The Genealogical Society or taken to the temples for sealings only; filed in orange labeled binders.

SECONDARY SOURCE OF TESTIMONY, testimony of an event by someone other than a participant or an eye-witness at some time after the event when the fallibility of memory could be a factor; see testimony.

sic., thus; so; as copied; used in brackets [sic] to show that the wording is precisely reproduced.

SOCIAL AND COMMERCIAL JURISDICTION, a sphere of authority; includes all records except those originating in the home, ecclesiastical, or civil jurisdictions; see jurisdiction.

SOCIAL AND COMMERCIAL RECORD CATEGORY, an arbitrary grouping of records; includes only records from the social and commercial jurisdiction; see record category.

STACKS, see library stacks.

STAKE, L.D.S. CHURCH, a geographic division outside the mission field; divided into wards, independent branches, and/or dependent branches.

STATUS FAMILY GROUP RECORD, up-to-date family group record.

SURNAME CARD INDEX, an index of names of persons compiled from parts of books or records at the library of The Genealogical Society; an analytic card index.

SURVEY PHASE, includes searching (1) home jurisdiction, (2) certain printed secondary records, and (3) L.D.S. Church jurisdiction; the objective is to lay a foundation for the research phase.

T.I.B., see Temple Records Index Bureau.

TEMPLE ORDINANCES, L.D.S. CHURCH, of concern in genealogy: baptism, endowment, sealing of couples (wife to husband), and sealing of families (children to parents).

TEMPLE RECORDS INDEX BUREAU (T.I.B.), contains a church-wide index to endowments; a department of The Genealogical Society.

TESTIMONY, declaration or statement made to establish proof or fact; may be oral or documentary.

TRADITION, oral testimony which has been passed verbally from one generation to another.

UNFINISHED SECTION, family group records for which ordinance dates are not complete; a part of the Main Records Section of the Church Records Archives; filed in white labeled binders.

UTAH IMMIGRATION CARD INDEX (1847-1868), a card index of names of pioneer immigrants to Utah; variously referred to as Crossing the Plains Card Catalogue, Crossing the Plains

Card Index, Crossing the Plains, Pioneer Card Catalogue, Emigrations Crossing the Plains, and Company List Index.

VITAL RECORD CATEGORY (civil), an arbitrary grouping of records; includes records of birth, marriage, death, and divorce kept by authorities in the civil jurisdiction or government; see record category.

WARD, L.D.S. CHURCH, a geographic division within a stake.

WITNESS, an individual whose knowledge of a fact or occurrence is sufficient to testify in respect to it.

ANNOTATED BIBLIOGRAPHY

General genealogical references are cited which contain information about the following: (1) basic genealogical terminology and procedures; (2) research tools, such as notekeeping, indexing materials, compiling a Family Record Book, forming a family organization, and general library usage; (3) sources from the jurisdiction of The Church of Jesus Christ of Latter-day Saints and early Utah; (4) genealogical teaching manuals prepared by The Church of Jesus Christ of Latter-day Saints; and (5) information on the doctrines of The Church of Jesus Christ of Latter-day Saints concerning genealogical research and temple work. Each reference cited has been examined to be certain it contains some of the foregoing information. For this reason this bibliography contains only references available to the authors at the Brigham Young University Library and the library of The Genealogical Society of The Church of Jesus Christ of Latter-day Saints, Inc. References containing only information on the research phase have not been included.

Allaben, Frank. *Concerning Genealogies.* New York: The Grafton Press, 1904.
    Descriptions of genealogical research as a hobby along with the satisfaction of doing such work; suggestions for compiling and printing genealogies.

Arizona Temple District. Genealogical Library. *Know How Book.* Mesa, Arizona: 1953.

Quotations from L.D.S. Church leaders on reasons for doing genealogical research; miscellaneous descriptions of record sources, pedigrees, family group examples, pedigree indexes, family organizations, and locality research in the United States and England.

Arizona Temple District. Genealogical Library. *Practical Research in Genealogy.* Mesa, Arizona: Lofgreen Printing and Office, 1955.

Information on research by correspondence and on the value of original sources; good descriptions of record sources in the United States and some foreign countries; historical maps.

Bancroft, Hubert Howe. *History of Utah.* Salt Lake City: Bookcraft, 1964.

One of the better histories of Utah; dates from 1840 to 1885; the story of Mormonism and migration of the Mormons; well documented.

Bennett, Archibald F. *Family Exaltation.* Salt Lake City: Deseret Sunday School Union Board, Deseret News Press, 1959.

Sunday School lesson manual explaining how the family relates to the Plan of Salvation; suggestions for writing personal and family histories; case examples in genealogical research and suggested sources to search for accurate records.

Bennett, Archibald F. *Genealogy Work, It's History, Purpose, and Destiny.* An address to Seminary and Institute Faculty. Provo, Utah: Brigham Young University Press, 1958.

The history and doctrines of genealogical research.

Bennett, Archibald F. *A Guide for Genealogical Research.* 2d. ed.: Salt Lake City: The Genealogical Society of The Church of Jesus Christ of Latter-day Saints, 1960.

Miscellaneous record sources, including L.D.S. Church records; information on libraries, microfilms, planning research, analyzing and evaluating sources; glossary of genealogical terms, foreign words with translations, information on research in foreign countries, samples of early handwriting, listing of libraries and historical societies, and data on calendar changes.

Bennett, Archibald F. *Methods of Tracing Pedigrees.* Salt Lake City: Genealogical Society of Utah, 1936.
Forty introductory lessons to train members of the L.D.S. Church in genealogical research; examples of results of searches; data on L.D.S. Church record sources; case examples; and family stories.

Bennett, Archibald F. *Proving Your Pedigree.* Salt Lake City: Deseret Sunday School Union Board, 1951.
Instructions on beginning a personal history, use of various records in America; research in foreign countries; and many case examples and personal histories.

Bennett, Archibald F. *Saviours on Mount Zion.* Salt Lake City: The Deseret News Press, 1950.
Collection of sermons and writings of various Church authorities; brief description of some research tools and methods; interesting faith promoting experiences.

Bennett, Archibald F. *Searching With Success.* Salt Lake City: Deseret Book Co., 1962.
Explains the Plan of Salvation and the obligation of the living to the dead; various sources with illustrations of their use by case example.

Bennion, Howard S. *Genealogical Research, A Practical Mission.* Salt Lake City: Deseret News Press. 1964.
Sunday School lesson manual with a variety of genealogical infomation; brief information on research in various countries.

Biographical Record of Salt Lake City and Vicinity. Chicago: Natural Historical Record Co., 1902.
Excellent genealogical data in biographical form; no index; not alphabetical.

Brace, William Raymond. *The Utah Genealogical Society*. Chicago: The University of Chicago Press, 1956.
Written as a Master's thesis; does not tell how to do research, mainly a survey of the library patrons as to age, residence, etc.; a history of The Genealogical Society; out-dated.

Cache Genealogical Library, Logan, Utah. *Handbook for Genealogical Correspondence*. Salt Lake City: Bookcraft, 1963.
Valuable text on how and where to write letters for genealogical information; ideas on information available by correspondence; sample letters, addresses, proper titles, and forms of address. The appendix lists libraries in the United States and their services, available maps, and a bibliography.

Carter, Kate B. *Heart Throbs of the West*. Vols. 1-12. Salt Lake City: Daughters of Utah Pioneers, 1939-1951.
Compiled from monthly pamphlets issued with the same title; biographies of many pioneers and early Utahns; historical accounts of Utah. An index has been compiled by Beth Oyler, Salt Lake City, 1948, 75pp.

Carter, Kate B. *Treasures of Pioneer History*. Vols. 1-5. Salt Lake City: Daughters of Utah Pioneers, 1952-
Historical accounts of early Utah; biographies of pioneers and early Utahns.

Christensen, Ross. T. "The Latter-day Saint Family Organization" (unpublished research paper, Brigham Young University, 1946.)
Includes a definition of terms; case example of the Young family; some L.D.S. Church doctrine.

Christenson, Harold T. and Bennett, Archibald F. *The Latter-day Saint Family*. Salt Lake City: Deseret Sunday School Union Board, 1946.
Genealogical training manual for youth; emphasis on celestial marriage and how to begin genealogical research. Contents: Section 1. "The Church and Modern Marriage." Section 2. "The Eternal Family."

The Church of Jesus Christ of Latter-day Saints. *Genealogical Information for Missionary and Convert*, n.p., n.d.
Suggestions for beginning genealogical research; emphasizes the importance of the missionary teaching the convert; outdated instructions for recording information on the family group record.

The Church of Jesus Christ of Latter-day Saints. *Priesthood Genealogy Handbook*. Salt Lake City: 1964.
Handbook for officers of the Priesthood responsible for genealogical research and temple work.

The Church of Jesus Christ of Latter-day Saints. The Priesthood Genealogy Committee. *Branch Libraries of the Genealogical Society of The Church of Jesus Christ of Latter-day Saints, Inc.* Salt Lake City: 1965.
Instructions for organizing and maintaining a branch library of The Genealogical Society.

The Church of Jesus Christ of Latter-day Saints. *Genealogy in Action*. Salt Lake City: 1964.
Teaching manual for M.I.A. workshop classes; information on notekeeping, family organizations, basic research procedures, libraries, and L.D.S. Church record sources.

The Church of Jesus Christ of Latter-day Saints. *Priesthood Correlation in the Genealogy Program*. Salt Lake City: 1964.
Manual to instruct Priesthood members in the relationship of genealogy to the general Priesthood correlation program; some information on The Genealogical Society, the value of a family organization, and the responsibility of the individual in genealogical research.

Crofton, H. A. *How to Trace a Pedigree*. London: Elliot Stock, 1911.
Basic hints for beginners; majority of information concerns English record sources.

Deseret Sunday School Union Board. *Adventures in Research.* Salt Lake City: 1943.
Lessons on sources in various countries; personal histories and case examples.

Deseret Sunday School Union Board. *Birthright Blessings.* Salt Lake City: 1942.
Teachings of the Prophets concerning the birthright of Israel; the celestial family order; and reasons for genealogical and temple work.

Deseret Sunday School Union Board. *Out of the Books.* Salt Lake City: 1940.
Doctrinal explanations on genealogy and temple work; various information on record sources, libraries, L.D.S. Church record sources, and family histories; good data on family organizations.

Doan, Gilbert H. *Search for Your Ancestors.* New York: McGraw-Hill, 1948.
A general approach to genealogical research with particular emphasis on United States research; case examples; mention of some printed sources.

The Doctrine and Covenants of The Church of Jesus Christ of Latter-day Saints. Salt Lake City, Utah: Deseret Book Co.
Includes revelations given to Joseph Smith, The Prophet, on the importance of identifying ancestors and performing ordinances for them.

Esshom, Frank. *Pioneers and Prominent Men of Utah.* Salt Lake City: Utah Pioneers Book Publishing Co., 1913.
Pictures and biographies of many pioneers of Utah.

Everton, George B. and Rasmusson, Gunnar. *The New How Book.* 7th ed. Logan, Utah: Everton Publishers, 1965.
Instructions given on how to begin research; hints on preserving photographs, how to conduct a personal visit; research and record sources; a glossary of common genealogical terms; a valuable beginning handbook.

Fowler, William Chauncey. *Conditions of Success in Genealogical Investigations and Illustrations in the Character of Nathaniel Chauncey.* Boston: New England Historic-Genealogical Society, 1846.

Uses the life and character of Nathaniel Chauncey to explain the conditions of success in genealogical research: (1) love of kindred, (2) love for investigation, (3) active imagination, (4) sound and disciplined judgment, and (5) conscientious regard for truth.

Freedman, Paul. *The Principles of Scientific Research.* New York: Pergamon Press, 1960.

Definitions, history, and methods of research; sections on planning research and nature of research most helpful.

Gardner, David E., Harland, Derek, and Smith, Frank. *A Basic Course in Genealogy, Vol. I.* Salt Lake City: Bookcraft, 1958.

Written as an introduction to record keeping and research; data on completing genealogical forms out-dated; information on L.D.S. Church record sources.

Gates, Susa Young. *Surname Book and Racial History.* Salt Lake City: General Board of the Relief Society, 1918.

Miscellaneous data on origin of surnames in several localities; alphabetical list of surnames; section on libraries.

Genealogical and Historical Magazine of the Arizona Temple District. I–XXIII (1925–1946).

Information on temple work and genealogy with some L.D.S. Church history; reprints of talks by L.D.S. Church authorities.

Genealogical Associates. *Genealogy and Local History: An Archival and Bibliographical Guide.* 2d. rev ed.: Evanston, Ill.: n.p., 1959.

Basic ideas for learning local and family history; mentions record sources, where to purchase genealogical books, addresses of societies; and research in various countries.

Genealogical Association of the Church of Jesus Christ of Latter-day Saints. *Genealogical Executive Handbook*. Salt Lake City: 1962.

Instructions on forming a workable stake and ward genealogical committee; out-dated.

Genealogical Association of the Church of Jesus Christ of Latter-day Saints. *Genealogical Instruction Manual*. Salt Lake City: 1962.

Instructions on completing family group records for submission to the Genealogical Society; information on L.D.S. Church record sources, calendar changes, foreign terms, and Latin names. Section 14 out-dated as to proper abbreviations; but, is valuable for establishing jurisdictions and proper recording of places in foreign countries.

The Genealogical Society of The Church of Jesus Christ of Latter-day Saints. *Genealogical Instruction Manual*. Salt Lake City, 1965.

Instructions on properly recording information on the family group record for submission to The Genealogical Society; several supplements.

The Genealogical Society of The Church of Jesus Christ of Latter-day Saints. *The Genealogical Researcher*. Vol. I, No. 1-Vol. II, No.1. Salt Lake City: January, 1962-February, 1963.

Monthly bulletin published by the Presidency of The Genealogical Society to inform the stakes and wards of the genealogical program of the L.D.S. Church.

The Genealogical Society of The Church of Jesus Christ of Latter-day Saints. *Genealogy Pamphlets*. Salt Lake City: 1962.

Contents: 1. Genealogy, Yes But Why? 2. Genealogy, Yes But How? 3. First Steps in Genealogy. 4. Teamwork Through a Family Organization. 5. Don't Start Research: Until. 6. Need Help . . . to Prevent Duplication of Research? 7. Read Any Good Books Lately? 8. Letters! Letters! Letters! 9. Preparing Records for the Temples. 10. Names to the Temples.

The Genealogical Society of The Church of Jesus Christ of Latter-day Saints. *Handbook for Genealogy and Temple Work.* Salt Lake City: The Deseret News Press, 1952-1956.

A compilation of facts concerning genealogical research in the L.D.S. Church, its history and present status; some L.D.S. Church record sources mentioned; information varies with each edition.

The Genealogical Society of Utah. *Articles of Association and By-Laws of the Genealogical Society of Utah.* Salt Lake City: n.d.

The Genealogical Society of Utah. *A Book of Remembrance.* Salt Lake City: 1936.

First year junior genealogical course ideas concerning a life story, gathering pictures, writing letters, and doing temple baptisms.

The Genealogical Society of Utah. *Children of the Covenant.* Salt Lake City: 1937.

Lesson book for junior genealogical classes; explains pre-existence, Plan of Salvation, and reasons for doing genealogical research; emphasis on lineage and race with some tales and traditions to support the belief in the scattering of Israel.

The Genealogical Society of Utah. *Church Service on Genealogical Committees,* Salt Lake City: 1935.

Information on how to organize and operate a genealogical committee; ideas for teaching groups and encouraging temple activity; out-dated.

The Genealogical Society of Utah. *Discussion Themes for Class Studies of "The Progress of Man."* Salt Lake City: n.d.

Study guide to accompany Joseph Fielding Smith's, *The Progress of Man;* lessons in genealogy about 1937-1940.

The Genealogical Society of Utah. *The Forefather Quest.* Salt Lake City: 1937.

Lesson book for third year junior genealogical classes; history and doctrines of genealogy and temple work; many personal experiences; list of suggested activities for an award sheet.

The Genealogical Society of Utah. *A Guide for Leaders in Temple Work and Genealogy.* Salt Lake City: 1929.
Instructions for teachers in the L.D.S. Church on the importance of genealogical research and temple work.

The Genealogical Society of Utah. *Handbook of Genealogy and Temple Work.* Salt Lake City: 1924-1951.
Doctrines of the L.D.S. Church concerning genealogy and temple work; present programs of The Church; explanations of record sources in the United States and foreign countries; information varies with each edition; out-dated.

The Genealogical Society of Utah. *How We Can Help You.* Salt Lake City: n.d.
Information on services available at library of The Genealogical Society; out-dated.

The Genealogical Society of Utah. *Lessons in Genealogy.* 4th ed. Salt Lake City: 1921.
Information on reasons for genealogical research in the L.D.S. Church; basic research sources; hints on library research; organizing the family.

The Genealogical Society of Utah. *Methods of Genealogical Research.* Salt Lake City: 1934.
Lessons for junior and senior genealogical classes; information on family group records, home sources, L.D.S. Church record sources, and correspondence.

The Genealogical Society of Utah. *Our Lineage.* Salt Lake City: 1933.
Lessons for junior and senior genealogical classes on Israelite lineage, history of races, how to trace a lineage, and use of general record sources.

The Genealogical Society of Utah. *Power from on High.* Salt Lake City: 1937.
Lessons for fourth year junior genealogical classes; doctrines of genealogical research and temple work; examples of successful searches; suggested activities for an award sheet.

The Genealogical Society of Utah. *Seeking After Our Dead, Our Greatest Responsibility.* Salt Lake City: 1928.
Problems for discussion on why we seek our dead, where we seek, and how we seek; excellent doctrinal explanations on redemption of the dead; information on basic sources in United States, foreign countries, and L.D.S. Church records.

The Genealogical Society of Utah. *Teaching One Another.* Salt Lake City: 1938.
Hints on teaching genealogy in the home; details on writing biographies; examples of biographies; some data on locality searches; narrative form, illustrating a family situation.

The Genealogical Society of Utah. *Topical Outlines to "The Way to Perfection."* Salt Lake City: n.d.
Study guide to accompany Joseph Fielding Smith's, *The Way to Perfection;* lessons in genealogy about 1937-1940.

Hafen, LeRoy R., and Hafen, Ann. *Handcarts to Zion.* Glendale, California: Arthur H. Clark Co., 1960.
An account of the ten handcart companies, 1856-1860; journals, reports, and rosters of the handcart companies.

Harland, Derek. *Genealogical Research Standards.* Salt Lake City: Bookcraft, 1963.
Formerly, *A Basic Course in Genealogy, Vol. II.* Information on evaluating evidence, research procedures, and pedigree analysis; a description of the various sources available in the United States, England, and Scandinavia.

History of the Church of Jesus Christ of Latter-day Saints. Vols. I-VII. Salt Lake City: Deseret Book Co, 1950.
First six volumes written by Joseph Smith; seventh volume compiled from Brigham Young's notes and manuscripts; introduction and notes by Brigham H. Roberts; indexed.

Jacobus, Donald Lines. *Genealogy as a Pastime and Profession.* New Haven, Conn.: The Tuttle, Morehouse, and Taylor Co., 1930.

Many fine examples of what the professional researcher will encounter in his work; words of warning to those who wish to hire a professional researcher; information on printed secondary sources, and on original sources, with emphasis on New England; worthwhile reading for both the amateur and the professional genealogist.

Jakeman, James T. *Daughters of Utah Pioneers and their Mothers.* Western Album Publishing Co., 1916.
Excellent genealogical data in biographical form; portraits; no index; not alphabetical.

Jenson, Andrew. *Church Chronology.* Salt Lake City: Deseret News, 1914.
A chronological listing of certain important events in The Church of Jesus Christ of Latter-day Saints; first publication covers years 1805-1898; 1st supplement 1899-1905; and 2nd supplement, 1906-1913.

Jenson, Andrew. *Day by Day With The Utah Pioneers, 1847.* Salt Lake City: 1934.
A chronological record of the trek across the plains first published in the Salt Lake Tribune April 5, 1897 to July 24, 1897; map marking each stopping place of 1847; very complete; biographical data on some leaders; index to biographies.

Jenson, Andrew. *Encyclopedic History of the Church of Jesus Christ of Latter-day Saints.* Salt Lake City: Deseret News Publishing Co., 1941.
Alphabetical listing of histories of missions of The Church of Jesus Christ of Latter-day Saints and the organized stakes of Zion with their wards and branches; excellent for establishing organization dates of wards and branches.

Jenson, Andrew. *The Historical Record.* Vols. 1-9. Salt Lake City: 1886.
A monthly periodical devoted to historical, biographical, chronological, and statistical matters in The Church of Jesus Christ of Latter-day Saints.

Jenson, Andrew. *History of the Scandinavian Mission.* Salt Lake City: Deseret News Press, 1927.
Compiled from historical records kept in the Scandinavian Mission.

Jenson, Andrew. *Latter-day Saint Biographical Encyclopedia.* Vols. 1-4. Salt Lake City: The Andrew Jenson History Co., 1901-1936.
Biographical sketches of prominent men and women of The Church of Jesus Christ of Latter-day Saints.

Jones, Milton Jenkins. *Genealogical Research Work Book.* Salt Lake City: LDS Aids, 1965.
Hints on notekeeping and organizing research materials; a step-by-step jurisdictional approach with emphasis on research in the United States.

Jones, Ivie (Huish). *Saviours on Mount Zion.* El Paso, Texas: 1958.
A play written for genealogical teachers.

Jones, Vincent L. *Stamp Out Chaos! Eliminate Confusion.* An Address to The Mount Hood Genealogical Forum. Mount Hood, Oregon: 1963.
Excellent information on how to organize a research notekeeping system; definition of the basic survey; general information on research in the United States.

Kendall, Henry. *Kinship of Men.* London: Kegan, Paul, Trench Co., 1888.
Lengthy definitions on ancestry, posterity, brotherhood; reasons for the mixing of races.

Kirkham, E. Kay. *A to Z at the Library.* Salt Lake City: Deseret Book Co., 1958.
Instructions on use of the library of The Genealogical Society with a description of departments and services; out-dated.

Kirkham, E. Kay. *Photography in Genealogy: An Explanation of the O-Kay System of Record Keeping.* Salt Lake City; n.p. 1958.

Ideas for copying genealogical records via camera and tape recorder.

Knight, Hattie M. *The 1-2-3 Guide to Libraries.* Provo, Utah: Brigham Young University Press, 1964.
Text for orientation classes in library science; valuable as a self-instruction manual.

The Latter-day Saint Millenial Star. Vol. I- Manchester (and other cities), England: The British Mission of the Church of Jesus Christ of Latter-day Saints, 1840-
Information on L.D.S. Church doctrines; excerpts of talks given by Church authorities in England; early editions valuable for history of L.D.S. Church migrations; index prepared by Beth Oyler.

Leadership Lectures. Provo, Utah: Brigham Young University Press, 1934.
Lectures on scriptural background for genealogical research, library facilities, and sources in the United States and foreign countries.

Local History and Genealogical Society. *Handbook of Seminars in Genealogical Research.* Dallas, Texas: B. and W. Printing and Letter Service, 1964.
Reprint of lectures given at a series of research seminars; basic introduction to research with information on library searches in the United States.

Lundwall, N. B. *Temples of the Most High.* Salt Lake City: Bookcraft, 1952.
A history and physical description of modern temples; a brief history and description of the temple endowment; concordance on temples, temple references, and ordinances; bibliography; illustrations.

Mears, Neal F. *What is up in Your Family Tree?* Chicago: n.p., 1928.

Information on why persons do genealogical research; how to prepare for research; home sources; arranging data; professional vs. amateur.

Morris, Louise Elizabeth Burton. *Primer in Genealogical Research.* Dallas, Texas: B. and W. Printing and Letter Service, 1965.
Genealogical terms; importance of geography in genealogy; how to write a family history; origin of names; heraldry and coats of arms; sources in United States and England.

Nibley, Preston. *Exodus to Greatness.* Salt Lake City: Deseret News Press, 1947.
A day by day account of the Mormon migration from Nauvoo to Great Salt Lake Valley in 1847.

Office of the Church Historian. "Guide to the Historian's Office Library-Archives." Salt Lake City: The Church of Jesus Christ of Latter-day Saints, 1966.
Information regarding services and records in the Church Historian's Office.

Parker, Donald Dean. *Local History, How to Gather It, Write It, and Publish It.* New York: Social Science Research Council, 1944.
General information on library searches, consulting old residents, photographs, pictures, and details on many record sources; hints on publishing a history.

Perpetual Emigrating Fund Co. *Names of Persons and Sureties Indebted to the Perpetual Emigrating Fund Company from 1850 to 1877 Inclusive.* Salt Lake City: Star Book and Job Printing Office, 1877.
Names of persons who immigrated to Great Salt Lake Valley from various parts of the United States and from foreign countries with financial aid from the P.E. Fund Co.; gives arrival date.

Petersen, Mark E. "Your Family Tree," in *Handbook of the Restoration,* n.p., 1946, pp. 503, 512.

Phillimore, William Phillimore Watts, *How to Write the History of a Family, a Guide for the Genealogist.* Boston: Cupples and Hurd, 1888.
Ideas given for compiling data, records to search, and how to organize material.

Phillimore, William Phillimore Watts. *Pedigree Work.* 3d. ed. London: Phillimore and Co., Ltd., 1936.
Suggestions for beginning research, verifying references, and establishing good research habits.

Portrait, Genealogical and Biographical Record of the State of Utah. Chicago: National Historical Record Co., 1902.
Contains biographies and portraits of many well known Utah citizens.

Prince. William H. *Genealogical Work Shop.* Salt Lake City: Bookcraft, 1955.
Lesson manual with assignments on completing family group records; rulings of The Genealogical Society; out-dated.

Reed, Evan Laforrest. *Ways and Means of Identifying Ancestors.* Chicago: Ancestral Publishing and Supply Co., 1946.
Information on home sources, printed sources, and original sources; research in the United States.

Reed, Evan Laforrest. *Whence Came You and How to Provide the Answer.* Chicago: Ancestral Publishing and Supply Co., 1936.
Motives and methods of ancestral research; importance of home sources and original sources; research in the United States and foreign countries; case examples.

Roach, Delbert. "A Specialized Genealogical Collection." *Mountain Plains Library Quarterly.* IX (Spring, 1964), 23-25.
Information on the classification and cataloguing systems at the library of The Genealogical Society and services available to the public.

Rubincam, Milton, ed. *Genealogical Research Methods and Sources.*
Washington, D.C.: The American Society of Genealogists,
1961.
General genealogical data and definitions; information on
records in the United States, England, Canada, and Continental
Europe.

Rubincam, Milton, *The Tools and Techniques of Genealogical Research,* Washington, D.C.: Ace Reporting Co., 1954.
Need for skilled genealogists and the qualifications of a good
researcher; secondary sources and the need for accurate records.

Rye, Walter. *Records and Record Searching.* Boston: J. G. Cupples
and Co., 1888.
Hints on beginning research and making notes; majority devoted to English research.

Simmons, Ralph. *Utah's Distinguished Personalities.* Salt Lake City:
Personality Pub. Co., 1933.
Biographical directory of Utah citizens of 1932-1933; excellent
biographical data.

Smith, Joseph Fielding. *The Progress of Man.* Salt Lake City:
Deseret Book Co., 1964.
An outline of Man's history, written at the request of The
Genealogical Society of Utah; thoughts on divine government.

Smith, Joseph Fielding. *The Way to Perfection.* Salt Lake City:
Deseret News Press, 1951.
Faith-promoting discussions of doctrinal principles and historical theme illustrating the place of the redemption of the
dead in the life of the Latter-day Saint.

Stetson, Oscar Frank. *The Art of Ancester Hunting.* Battleboro,
Vt.: Stephen Daye Press, 1936.
General description of genealogy: suggestions for keeping
notes and searching sources; New England oriented.

Stevenson, J. Grant. "Development and Ramifications of Vicarious Work for the Dead in the L D.S. Church." Unpublished paper written at Brigham Young University, n.d.
Revelations and visions concerning the redemption of the dead given in chronological order beginning with 1830.

Stevenson, J. Grant. *Genealogical Society Rulings*. Provo, Utah: Stevenson Supply, 1962.
A discussion of rulings of The Genealogical Society of the L.D.S. Church concerning family group records, temple and family files, and computer symbols.

Stevenson, J. Grant. *A Genealogical Study Guide*. Provo, Utah: Stevenson Supply, 1962.
A bibliography of genealogical reference books; list of 694 questions to be answered by the genealogical student.

Stevenson, J. Grant. *A Genealogical Check List*. Provo, Utah: Stevenson Supply, 1964.
A step-by-step guide to the library of The Genealogical Society and the Church Historian's Office; bibliography of genealogical references; sample family group record and pedigree chart; hints on genealogical correspondence; how to write and compile family histories; suggestions for locating various genealogical materials.

Stevenson, J. Grant. *Research Aids*. Provo, Utah: Stevenson Supply, 1962.
A compilation of research sources and ideas for the United States, England, Canada, and Continental Europe; histories; addresses for public officials.

Stevenson, J. Grant. *A Trip Through the Files of Time*. Provo, Utah: Stevenson Supply, n.d.
Information on library of The Genealogical Society; out-dated.

Stevenson, Noel C. *The Genealogical Reader*. Salt Lake City: Deseret Book Co., 1958.

A collection of selected articles from various genealogical periodicals on identifying the immigrant ancestor, hiring professional genealogists, English traditions, Colonial American traditions, calendar changes, and genealogy as a science; valuable background data, but nothing specifically given on how to proceed with research.

Stevenson, Noel C. *Genealogy and the Right of Privacy.* n.p., 1948.
Gives the legal history of the "right of privacy" law and emphasizes that the right of privacy does not apply to the dead.

Stiles, Henry R. *A Handbook of Practical Suggestions for the Use of Students in Genealogy.* Albany, New York: Joel Munsell's Sons, 1899.
Excellent information on definitions and objectives of genealogical research; hints on notekeeping; record sources in the United States.

Sudweeks, Joseph. *Exercise Book for Principles and Practices of Genealogy.* Provo, Utah: Brigham Young University Press, 1952.
A set of questions for student study on the subject of genealogy.

Sudweeks, Joseph. *Kinship, One Kind of Relationship.* Provo, Utah: Brigham Young University Press, 1955.
A discussion of various relationships; direct, collateral, and cousinship; how to calculate relationships.

Sudweeks, Joseph. *The Principles and Practices of Genealogy.* Salt Lake City: Deseret Sunday School Union Board, 1950.
Miscellaneous record sources with information on The Genealogical Society, L.D.S. Church Records, the Plan of Salvation.

Talmage, James E. *The House of the Lord.* 3d. ed., Salt Lake City: Bookcraft, 1962.
History of temples and temple work in both ancient and modern times; excellent photographs and illustrations.

Tolman, William Odell. *An Introduction to Record Keeping and Research.* Provo, Utah: n.p., n.d.
Designed for 20 hours of teaching instruction in genealogical research; excellent bibliography of general references; L.D.S. Church doctrine; sample pedigree, family group record, and personal record; relationship chart; ideas for correspondence.

Tullidge, Edward W. *History of Salt Lake City.* Salt Lake City: Star Printing Company, 1886.
One of the better histories of Salt Lake City.

Tullidge, Edward W. *Women of Mormondom.* New York: Tullidge and Crandall, 1877.
Biographies, stories, and histories of L.D.S. Women; unindexed.

Tyler, Daniel. *A Concise History of the Mormon Battalion in the Mexican War, 1846-1847.* Chicago, Rio Grande Press Inc., 1964.
Reprint of the 1881 edition; information from private journals, diaries, etc.

The Utah Genealogical and Historical Magazine. Vols. I-XXXI. Salt Lake City: The Genealogical Society of Utah, 1910-October, 1940.
Lessons on genealogical research; valuable information on L.D.S. Church records and early Utah history.

The Utah Historical Quarterly. Vols. I- . Salt Lake City: The Utah State Historical Society, January 1, 1928-1933; December, 1938-
Information on Utah history and traditions; life sketches of prominent individuals.

Wadham, Rex A., and Memmott, Evan J. *Creative Genealogy.* Provo, Utah: Offset Copy Co., 1965.
Instructions on basic genealogical forms and how to prepare materials.

White, David, comp. *Instruction Manual for Genealogical Research.* Provo, Utah: Brigham Young University Press, 1952.

Prepared as an instruction manual for the Campus Branch Genealogical Committee; L.D.S. Church doctrines; instructions for completing pedigree charts and family group records; notekeeping suggestions and examples of research in the United States.

Widtsoe, John A. *Priesthood and Church Government in the Church of Jesus Christ of Latter-day Saints.* Rev. ed. Salt Lake City: Deseret Book Co., 1954.

History of the Priesthood and duties of the Priesthood bearers; principles of L.D.S. Church government; information on records kept by the L.D.S. Church.

Williams, Ethel W. *Know Your Ancestors.* Rutland, Vt.: Charles E. Tuttle, 1960.

General genealogical reference; hints on using home sources, library usage, research in the United States and some foreign countries; glossary and bibliography.

Willis, Arthur James. *Introducing Genealogy.* London: Ernest Benn, 1961.

Information on beginning research in the home; suggestions for recording information; English oriented.

Yellowstone District Genealogy Committee. *Stepping Stones to Research.* Billings, Mont.: 1954.

Ten lessons on beginning research; and correspondence; appendix lists some libraries in the United States.

INDEX

Accredited Researcher,
    Sample Letter, 199-200.
    See also Genealogical Society of The
    Church of Jesus Christ of Latter-day
    Saints, Inc., Research Accreditation.
Agent, 196-97.
Ancestral Couple, 7; *see also* Family Org-
    anization, Selecting Ancestral Couple.
Annual Report, *see* Form E (annual re-
    port).
Archives, *see* Church Records Archives.
Assistance with the Survey, *see* Survey,
    Assistance with the.
Australia, 138.
Author Card, 71.

Baptism Dates, 103, 111, 160; *see also*
    Temple Ordinance Records; *see also*
    Temple Records Index Bureau.
Belgium, 138.
Bibliography, Annotated, 218-38.
Birth Certificates, *see* Delayed Birth Cer-
    tificates.
Bishop's Report of L.D.S. Church Mem-
    bers, 157-58, 160.
Book of Remembrance, *see* Family Record
    Book.
Branch Libraries, *see* Genealogical Society
    of The Church of Jesus Christ of
    Latter-day Saints, Inc., The.

C.H.O., *see* Church Historian's Office.
C.R.A., *see* Church Records Archives.
Calculation of Relationships, *see* relation-
    ships.
Calendar of Correspondence, *see* notekeep-
    ing.
Calendar of Search, *see* notekeeping.

Card Catalogue, 70-72.
Card Indexes, *see* index to.
Card-Indexed Pedigree Charts, 105; *see*
    Church Records Archives.
Cataloguing, *see* Library; *see* Genealogical
    Society of The Church of Jesus Christ of
    Latter-day Saints, Inc., The.
Cemetery Record Category, *see* Record
    Category.
Census Record Category, *see* Record Cate-
    gory.
Census Records, L.D.S. Church, *see*
    L.D.S. Church Census.
Chronology of Temple Ordinances, 184-85.
Church Historian's Office, 90.
    Address, 205.
Church of Jesus Christ of Latter-day
    Saints, The, 7, 37, 89.
    Administrative Authorities, 88-89.
    Geographic Divisions, 86-88.
    Office Address, 205.
    Organization, 86-89.
Church Records Archives, 95-96, 104,
    107-12.
    Availability, 110-11.
    Family Group Records, 108-10.
        Finished Section, 109, 111.
        Main Records Section, 109-10, 111.
        Miscellaneous, 109.
        Patrons Section, 109.
        Processed Section, 109.
        Sealing Section, 110.
        Unfinished Section, 109-10, 111.
    Genealogical Application, 111.
    Genealogical Limitations, 112.
    Pedigree Charts, 107-8.
        Alphabetized, 108.
        Card-indexed, 107-8.

Miscellaneous, 108.
Sample Letter, 198.
Church-Wide Membership File, 155, 159, 160.
Circumstantial Evidence, see evidence.
Civil (Government) Jurisdiction, see jurisdiction.
Classification, see Genealogical Society of The Church of Jesus Christ of Latter-day Saints, Inc., The; see library.
Client, 193-195.
Collateral Relationships, see relationships.
Commercial Firms, 195-96.
Company List Index, see Utah Immigration Card Index.
Copied Records, see testimony.
Correspondence, 197-200.
Accredited Researcher, 199-200.
Church Records Archives, 198.
Family Organization, 63.
Temple Records Index Bureau, 198, 199-200.
Court Record Category, see record category.
Cross Referencing Pedigree Charts, see pedigree chart.
Crossing the Ocean, see European Emigration Card Index.
Crossing the Plains, Crossing the Plains Card Catalogue, or Crossing the Plains Index, see Utah Immigration Card Index.

Dates, 3, 4, 7, 9, 15-16.
Hints for Recording, 15-16.
Months Indicated by Numerals, 15.
Death Registration, 176-77.
Deceased Members File, 155, 159, 160.
Delayed Birth Certificates (L.D.S. Church), 164, 165, 178-79.
Dewey Decimal Classification, 73, 91.
Direct Evidence, see evidence.
Discrepancies, 31, 32-33.
Documentary Testimony, see testimony.

Early Church Information Card Index, 115-17.
Early Church Information File, see Early Church Information Card Index.
Ecclesiastical (Church) Jurisdiction, see jurisdiction.
Ecclesiastical (Church) Record Category, see record category.
Elements of Identity, 4, 7, 9-20.
Emigration, see L. D. S. Church Emigration, Immigration, and Migration.
Emigration Card Catalogue, see European Emigration Card Index.
Emigration-Immigration Record Category, see record category.

Emigrations, Crossing the Plains, see Utah Immigration Card Index.
Emigration Records of Continental Europe, see Emigration Registers of Continental Europe.
Emigration Registers of Continental Europe, 141-44.
Emigration Registers of the British Mission, 136, 138-41.
Emigration Records of the British Mission, see Emigration Registers of the British Mission.
Endowment Dates, 103; see also Temple Ordinance Records; see also Temple Records Index Bureau.
European Emigration Card Index, 136-38, 141, 143.
Evidence, 3, 4, 28-33.
Circumstantial, 29.
Direct, 29.
Hearsay, 28.
Origin and evaluation, 28-33.
Summary, 31-32.

Family Group Record, 4, 6, 7, 28, 37, 50, 52, 53, 54, 59, 105.
Processing, 94-96.
Status, see notekeeping.
See also Church Records Archives.
Family Group Sheet, see Family Group Record.
Family Organization(s), 4, 59, 61-69, 97.
Contacting Family Members, 62-63.
Family Organization File, 97.
Genealogical Research, 67.
Objectives, 61.
Reorganizing a Family, 68-69.
Sample Constitution, 64-66.
Sample Letter, 63.
Selecting Ancestral Couple, 62.
Family Organization File, see Genealogical Society of The Church of Jesus Christ of Latter-day Saints, Inc., The; see Family Organization.
Family Record Book, 4, 37-51, 53.
Family Representative, 111, 188.
Film, see microfilm.
Finished Section, see Church Records Archives.
Form E (annual report), 152-54, 159, 160.
France, 138.

Genealogical Instruction Manual, 7.
Genealogical Research, 3, 37, 67.
Basic Steps, 4.
Method, 3, 4, 7.
Scientific, 3.
Specialist, 3, 192-93.
Tools, 4, 37, 61.

FUNDAMENTALS OF GENEALOGICAL RESEARCH

Land Record Category, see record category.
Large or Long Book, see Long or Large Book.
Library, 4, 70-77.
    Card Catalogue, 70-72.
    Classification, 73-74.
    Departments, 74-76.
Library, The Genealogical Society, see Genealogical Society Library, The
Lineal Relationships, see relationships.
Lines of Responsibility, see relationships.
Liverpool Office Emigration Records, see Emigration Registers of the British Mission.
Long or Large Book, 149-50, 159.

Main Records Section, see Church Records Archives.
Marriage License Card Index, 117-18.
Membership Card Index, 156-57, 160
Membership Records, see L. D. S. Church Records of Membership.
Microfilm, 92.
Migration, see L. D. S. Church Emigration, Immigration, and Migration.
Military Record Category, see record category.
Minnie Margetts' File, see Membership Card Index.
Miscellaneous Family Group Records, see Church Records Archives.
Miscellaneous Marriage Index, see Marriage License Card Index.
Mission Records, see Stake and Mission Records.
Missionary Records and Index, 172-74.

Names, 3, 4, 7, 9-14.
    Changes, 12.
    Customs and Traditions, 11-12.
    Origin, 9-11.
        Ancestral or Patronymic, 10-11.
        Occupational, 10.
        Personal Characteristic, 11.
        Place, 10.
    Spelling Variations, 12-14.
Notebook, see notekeeping, research notebook.
Notekeeping, 4, 52-60.
    Calendar of Correspondence, 56-57.
    Calendar of Search, 54-56, 57.
    Research Folder, 53-54.
    Research Notebook, 57-59.
    Status Family Group Record, 53.
    Summary, 59.
Numbering Individuals on Pedigree Charts, see pedigree chart.

Numbering Pedigree Charts, see pedigree chart.

Obituary Card Index, 119-20.
Obituary File or Index, see Obituary Card Index.
Oral Testimony, see testimony.
Original Record, 3; see also testimony.

P. B. O., see Presiding Bishop's Office.
P. R. S., see Genealogical Society of The Church of Jesus Christ of Latter-day Saints, Inc., The, Pedigree Referral Service.
Patriarchal Blessings, Card Index, 171-72.
Patrons Section, see Church Records Archives.
Partial Card Index, see Membership Card Index.
Passenger Lists, see Emigration Registers of the British Mission; see Emigration Registers of Continental Europe.
Patron, see client.
Pedigree Chart, 4, 5, 7, 28, 37-50, 52, 53, 105.
    Cross Referencing 48-49.
    Indexing, 50.
    Numbering Charts, 39-47.
    Numbering Individuals, 39.
    See also Church Records Archives.
Pedigree Referral Service, see Genealogical Society of The Church of Jesus Christ of Latter-day Saints, Inc., The.
Pioneer Card Catalogue, see Utah Immigration Card Index.
Places, 3, 4, 7, 9, 14-15.
    Errors, 14-15.
    Spelling Variations, 14.
Poland, 138.
Presiding Bishop's Office, 90.
    Address 213.
Priesthood Lineage, see Tracing Line of Authority of Ordination to the Priesthood.
Priesthood Quorum Records, 170-71.
Primary Source, 3, 105, 140, 143, 161, 166, 190; see also testimony.
Printed Secondary Record Category, see record category.
Probate Record Category, see record category.
Processed Section, See Church Records Archives.
Professional Genealogical Researcher, 53, 59.

Record Category, 21-27.
    Cemetery, 22, 24, 27.

Census, 22, 24-25, 27.
Court Record, 22, 25, 27.
Ecclesiastical (church), 22, 23-24, 27.
Emigration-immigration, 22, 26, 27.
Home, 22, 23, 27.
Land, 22, 25, 27.
Military, 22, 26, 27.
Printed Secondary, 7, 22, 23, 27 84-85.
Probate, 22, 25, 27.
Social and Commercial, 22, 26, 27.
Vital (civil), 22, 24, 27.
Records of Membership, see L.D.S. Church Records of Membership.
Relationships, 3, 4, 7, 9, 11, 16-20, 52.
Calculations, 17-20.
Collateral, 17, 19-20.
Lineal, 17-18.
Lines of Responsibility. 16-17.
Research, see genealogical research.
Research Department, see Genealogical Society of The Church of Jesus Christ of Latter-day Saints, Inc., The.
Research Folder, see notekeeping.
Research Notebook, see notekeeping.
Research Phase, 7, 21, 53, 59.

Salt Lake City Deaths, see death registration.
Salt Lake City Newspaper Obituaries, see Obituary Card Index.
Sample Letters,
Accredited Researcher, 199-200.
Church Records Archives, 198.
Family Organization, 63.
Temple Records Index Bureau, 198, 199-200.
Scandinavia, 138.
Sealing Dates, 104, 111; see also Temple Ordinance Records; see also Temple Records Index Bureau.
Sealing Section, see Church Records Archives.
Secondary Source, see testimony.
Seventies Quorum Records, 170.
Shipping File Index, see European Emigration Card Index.
Shipping Records, Emigrations by Ship, see Emigration Registers of the British Mission; see Emigration Registers of Continental Europe.
Social and Commercial Jurisdiction, see jurisdiction.
Social and Commericial Record Category, see record category.
Source of Testimony, see testimony.
South Africa, 138.
Stake and Mission Records,
Historical, 174-75.

Index to Manuscript Histories, 174-75.
Manuscript Histories, 174-75.
Status Family Group Record, see notekeeping.
Subject Card, 72.
Surname Card Index, 114-15.
Surname File, see Surname Card Index.
Surnames, see names.
Survey, Assistance with the, 192-200.
Survey Phase, 7, 21, 53, 54, 59, 81-85, 98, 105.
Switzerland, 138.

T. I. B., see Temple Records Index Bureau.
Temple Index Bureau, see Temple Records Index Bureau.
Temple Ordinance Chronology, 184-85.
Temple Ordinance Records, 111, 180-91.
Availability, 189.
Chronology of Temple Ordinances, 184-85.
Contents, 183-87.
Genealogical Application, 190.
Genealogical Limitations, 190.
Indexes, 187-89.
Origin, 181-83.

Temple Records Index Bureau, 95, 98-106, 106, 111.
Availability, 103.
Card, 99.
Contents, 99-103.
Genealogical Application, 103-5.
Genealogical Limitations, 105-6.
Origin, 98-99.
Sample Letter, 198, 199-200.
Testimony, 28-32.
Documentary, 30.
Copied, 30.
Original, 30.
Oral, 28, 29.
Source, 31-32.
Primary, 31.
Secondary, 31.
Summary, 31-32.
Title Card, 72.
Tracing Line of Authority of Ordination to the Priesthood, 161.
Triple-Indexed Book, 150-51, 159.

Unfinished Section, see Church Records Archives.
Utah Immigration Card Index, 134-36.

Vital (Civil) Record Category, see record category.

Ward and Branch Records, Historical, 175-76.